mo
simple chess

John Emms

EVERYMAN CHESS

Gloucester Publishers plc   www.everymanchess.com

First published in 2004 by Gloucester Publishers plc (formerly Everyman Publishers plc), Northburgh House, 10 Northburgh Street, London EC1V 0AT

British Library Cataloguing-in-Publication Data
A catalogue record for this book is available from the British Library.

ISBN 1 85744 343 8

Distributed in North America by The Globe Pequot Press, P.O Box 480, 246 Goose Lane, Guilford, CT 06437-0480.

All other sales enquiries should be directed to Everyman Chess, Northburgh House, 10 Northburgh Street, London EC1V 0AT
tel: 020 7253 7887 fax: 020 7490 3708
email: info@everymanchess.com
website: www.everymanchess.com

EVERYMAN CHESS SERIES (formerly Cadogan Chess)
Chief advisor: Garry Kasparov
Commissioning editor: Byron Jacobs

Typeset and edited by First Rank Publishing, Brighton.
Cover design by Horatio Monteverde.
Production by Navigator Guides.
Printed and bound in the United States by Versa Press.

CONTENTS

BIBLIOGRAPHY

Books

Simple Chess, John Emms (Everyman 2001)
Training for the Tournament Player, Mark Dvoretsky and Artur Yusupov (Batsford 1993)
Secrets of Modern Chess Strategy, John Watson (Gambit 1998)
Chess Strategy in Action, John Watson (Gambit 2003)
The Most Amazing Chess Moves of All Time, John Emms (Gambit 2000)
Improve Your Chess Now, Jonathan Tisdall (Cadogan 1997)
Dynamic Chess Strategy, Mihai Suba (Pergamon 1991)
Positional Play, Mark Dvoretsky and Artur Yusupov (Batsford 1996)
Bishop v Knight: the verdict, Steve Mayer (Batsford 1997)
Learn from the Grandmasters, Raymond Keene et al (Batsford 1975)
Tactical Chess Exchanges, Gennady Nesis (Batsford 1991)
Piece Power, Peter Wells, (Batsford 1994)
The Seven Deadly Chess Sins, Jonathan Rowson (Gambit 2000)

Periodicals, Magazines and Websites

Chess Informant
ChessBase Magazine
British Chess Magazine
New In Chess Magazine
The Week in Chess
Chess Today
Scottish Correspondence Chess Association website

Simple Chess, John Emms (Everyman 2001)
Training for the Tournament Player, Mark Dvoretsky and Artur Yusupov (Batsford 1993)
Secrets of Modern Chess Strategy, John Watson (Gambit 1998)
Chess Strategy in Action, John Watson (Gambit 2003)
The Most Amazing Chess Moves of All Time, John Emms (Gambit 2000)
Improve Your Chess Now, Jonathan Tisdall (Cadogan 1997)
Dynamic Chess Strategy, Mihai Suba (Pergamon 1991)
Positional Play, Mark Dvoretsky and Artur Yusupov (Batsford 1996)
Bishop v Knight: the verdict, Steve Mayer (Batsford 1997)
Learn from the Grandmasters, Raymond Keene et al (Batsford 1975)
Tactical Chess Exchanges, Gennady Nesis (Batsford 1991)
Piece Power, Peter Wells, (Batsford 1994)
The Seven Deadly Chess Sins, Jonathan Rowson (Gambit 2000)

INTRODUCTION

When I began gathering material for my earlier book *Simple Chess*, I soon realised that the number of aspects of positional play that especially appealed to me was quite substantial. Unfortunately, given the space limitations, it was just impossible to include all the topics of strategy that I had originally wished to. I overcame this problem to some extent by being very selective over what made it in and what didn't, but I wasn't totally happy at having to eliminate so much material. So, when the opportunity arose to write a follow-up to *Simple Chess*, I was very keen to do so. Thus you are reading an introduction to (the imaginatively titled) *More Simple Chess*!

While reading this book, some familiarity with *Simple Chess* might come in handy but it's certainly not essential. Nevertheless, for those of you who (for some mysterious reason) haven't been able to secure a copy of that book, here are a few 'snippets' that might prove to be useful:

1) An outpost is a square where it is possible to establish a piece that cannot easily be attacked by opposing pawns. All pieces like outposts, but often the best piece for an outpost is a knight.

2) A bishop is termed as 'good' when its pawns, especially the ones on the central files, do not obstruct its path. Likewise, a bishop is termed as 'bad' when its pawns, especially the ones on the central files, obstruct its path. However, these terms are a little misleading, as they don't necessarily reflect the actual effectiveness of a bishop. A 'good bishop' is often very effective, but can on occasions be very ineffective. At the same time, a 'bad bishop' is often just plain bad, but it *can* be very effective too, both in attack and for defensive purposes.

3) The 'bishop pair' (or the two bishops) often outweigh the 'bishop and knight' team, especially in the endgame.

4) Pawn weaknesses often become more apparent as pieces are exchanged.

5) More often than not, the player with more space is advised to refrain from exchanges that would otherwise seem fair. Conversely, the player with less space is advised to seek exchanges in order to reduce the effect of cramped pieces.

Now a brief run through the chapters of *More Simple Chess*. I've begun with a look at 'problem pieces', including examples of both how to improve your own and exploit your opponent's. Subjects dealt with here include 'power plays' and 'inducement'.

In Chapter Two, the longest in this book, I've considered the extremely broad topic of exchanges which, with one or two notable exceptions, hasn't been treated especially thoroughly in previous works. I'm not quite sure why this has been the case; perhaps it's because what I would consider a very important strategical subject isn't generally regarded as overly exciting material for chess literature (as GM Peter Wells pointed out, editors are much fonder of the word 'sacrifice' than 'exchange').

The final four chapters deal with the different pieces in turn. In Chapter Three I revisit the age-old subject of the struggles between the bishop pair and the 'bishop and knight' pairing, expanding on the ideas covered in *Simple Chess*. Also in this chapter I take a look at those 'hard-to-see' knight retreats, a concept that I'm particularly fond of.

In Chapter Four I study the queen, the most powerful piece on the chessboard. Included in this chapter are aspects of queen play that I believe haven't received much coverage before, like 'After eating the poisoned pawn: fighting or running away?' and 'Replacing the bishop'.

In Chapter Five it's the turn of the most valuable piece: the king. Here I concentrate on examples of king power in the endgame and the perennial question of if, when and where to castle.

Chapter Six deals with rooks. One subject that particularly appeals to me is the activation of the rooks along their 'home' files (the a- and h-files) and I've paid special attention to this feature.

I've tried to reflect the changes that have occurred in modern chess. In general I've also strived to include examples where the players must make really tough decisions; I'm less interested in cases where it's obvious to the majority what should be done and what should be avoided. In this respect I believe this book is more advanced than *Simple Chess*. You'll find that some of the examples contain surprising and somewhat paradoxical moves, even though they may well be the correct choices.

How can one improve his or her positional understanding of chess? What worked for me was the study of ideas in countless grandmaster games, plus playing hundreds (thousands?) of competitive games myself. If that sounded quite time-consuming, then I can assure you that it was! My hope is that you'll find the examples and exercises in this book instructive, challenging and entertaining, and that they can guide you to some extent on what to look out for in games and study.

Finally, many thanks go to both Byron Jacobs and Dan Addelman at Everyman Chess for their patience over deadlines.

John Emms,
Kent,
April 2004

CHAPTER ONE

Problem Pieces

Having to deal with ineffective pieces (I've called them problem pieces) is a perennial problem for the chess player, whether it is trying to make the best out of your own or attempting to subdue or exploit your opponent's. It's very difficult to make every piece happy – pawn structures will always dictate that some pieces are in a better mood than others and these pawn structures are usually determined by our choice of openings. For example, if Black plays the French Defence (1 e4 e6 2 d4 d5) or the Stonewall Dutch (1 d4 f5 followed by ...e7-e6, ...d7-d5 and ...c7-c6), the bishop on c8 has most reason to complain, while in certain closed lines of the Ruy Lopez (1 e4 e5 2 ♘f3 ♘c6 3 ♗b5 a6 4 ♗a4 ♘f6 5 0-0 ♗e7 6 ♖e1 b5 7 ♗b3 d6 8 c3 0-0 9 h3 ♘a5 10 ♗c2 c5 11 d4 ♘c6 12 d5 ♘a5 13 b3!, for example) it's Black's queen's knight that doesn't look happy.

What's important is how these problems are dealt with and in this chapter I'd like to expand on my thoughts in *Simple Chess*. There are three different aspects of 'problem pieces' that I'd like to look at, which are:

1) Improving your worst placed piece
2) Power plays
3) Inducement

Improving your worst placed piece

In positions of strategic manoeuvring (where time is not of decisive importance) seek the worst placed piece. Activating that piece is often the most reliable way of improving your position as a whole. – Dvoretsky

A very sensible tip, whether it's meant for advanced players (to which the famous and well-respected chess coach Mark Dvoretsky was aiming his advice), or simply absolute beginners. It's surprising, though, how often this advice is wrongly ignored. Players have a tendency to forget about their ineffective pieces until a concrete problem concerning that piece arises, preferring to concentrate on making the most of their more active ones. However, by the time a specific problem occurs, it may be too late do rectify matters. Instead it's often worth taking time out earlier on to look for a solution.

Let's begin with what I would consider a straightforward example of improving a piece, although perhaps this is only so because I've seen the manoeuvre in question so many times (sometimes to my own cost!).

Hagarova-Gleizerov
Cappelle la Grande 1995
French Defence

1 e4 e6 2 d4 d5 3 ♘d2 ♘f6 4 e5 ♘fd7 5 c3 c5 6 ♗d3 ♘c6 7 ♘e2 cxd4 8 cxd4 f6 9 exf6 ♛xf6 10 ♘f3 h6 11 0-0 ♗d6 12 ♘c3 0-0 13 a3 ♖d8 14 ♗c2 ♘f8 15 ♖e1

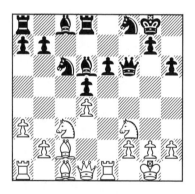

Here Black's worst placed piece is the bishop on c8, which is severely inhibited by the pawn on e6. The thrust ...e6-e5 would liberate the bishop, but this advance is difficult to arrange without leaving Black with central weaknesses. Instead Gleizerov carries out a typical plan associated with this type of position arising from the French Defence. In this particular case it works perfectly.

15...♗d7! 16 ♗e3 ♗e8!

Simple and yet so effective: the bishop can be introduced into the action with either ...♗g6, offering to exchange White's 'good bishop', or the more ambitious ...♗h5, pinning the f3-knight and adding further pressure to the isolated d4-pawn. What more could Black ask for from this once unfortunate piece?

17 ♖c1?

Completely underestimating the strength of Black's threats. I feel that White should already be looking to equalise, and one possible way would be 17 ♛d2 ♗h5 18 ♗d1!, unpinning and giving the knight on f3 some much needed protection.

17...♗h5!

Naturally!

18 ♗b1 ♖d7! 19 ♘a4 ♖f7 20 ♘c5 ♛e7

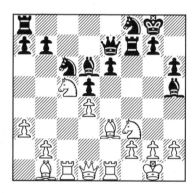

From being the worst placed piece on the board, Black's light-squared bishop has emerged as a major player in Black's now undoubted advantage. Gleizerov goes on to win very convincingly.

21 ♘d3 ♘g6! 22 ♛c2 ♗xf3 23 gxf3 ♖f5 24 f4 ♛h4 25 ♛e2 ♗xf4 26 ♘xf4 ♘xf4 27 ♗xf4 ♘xd4 28 ♛e3 ♖xf4 29 ♔h1 ♖xf2 30 ♛e5 ♛g4 0-1

This plan of ...♗c8-d7-e8 is a crucial weapon for Black to activate his theoretically 'bad' bishop in openings such as the French and the Dutch Stonewall.

In the next example we see two separate occasions within a few moves in which the same player improves his overall position just by repositioning his worst placed piece.

Tseshkovsky-Romanishin
Tallinn 1979
Ruy Lopez

1 e4 e5 2 ♘f3 ♘c6 3 ♗b5 a6 4 ♗a4 ♘f6 5 0-0 ♗e7 6 ♖e1 b5 7 ♗b3 d6 8 c3 0-0 9 d4 ♗g4 10 d5 ♘a5 11 ♗c2 ♕c8 12 h3 ♗d7 13 ♘bd2 c6 14 b4 ♘b7 15 dxc6 ♕xc6 16 ♗b2

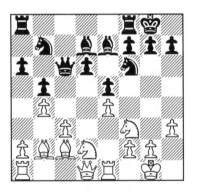

Romanishin realises that the position is reasonably quiet in nature and this gives him the time to improve the queen's knight. At the moment it is horribly placed on b7, where it is dominated by the b4-pawn.

16...♘d8!

It all looks quite transparent once the idea is comprehended – Black's knight is heading for the much greener pastures of e6 and f4. However, how many players would actually come up with an opening move of ...♘d8 here? A knight retreat is not the first move that comes to mind (see Chapter 3 for more on this), especially when Black has so many other reasonable-looking alternatives.

17 ♗d3 ♘e6 18 c4 ♕b7 19 a3 ♘f4 20 ♗f1 ♖ac8 21 ♖c1 ♗c6 22 g3 ♘e6 23 cxb5 axb5 24 ♗d3

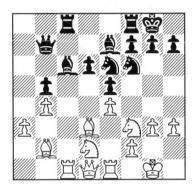

Once again it's time for Black to improve his worst placed piece. This time it's the passively placed bishop on e7.

24...♗d8!

Again Romanishin is not afraid to use the back rank as a stepping stone.

25 ♕e2 ♗b6

Now the bishop has found a beautiful diagonal where it bears down on White's king. Black's pieces are harmoniously placed and Romanishin went on to convert his advantage.

Although I've used the following example before (albeit in a different context), it deserves as much exposure as possible. I can't find a more exquisite model of a player improving the position of his worst placed piece.

Oll-Hodgson
Groningen 1993

(see following diagram)

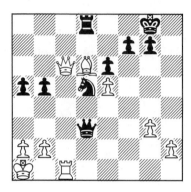

Let's examine the position as a whole from Black's point of view. The knight has a wonderful outpost on d5 and the queen is also well centralised on d3, where it patrols many squares and ties White's rook to the back rank. The only black piece not pulling its weight at the moment is the rook on d8, which is pretty much dominated by White's queen and bishop. If Black were able to activate this piece, then his positional advantages (stronger minor piece, better structure and light-squared dominance) would become decisive.

Only a player of Julian Hodgson's imagination could come up with such a profound solution to Black's problem.

34...♔h7!!

I voted this as one of my favourite moves of all time in my book *The Most Amazing Chess Moves of All Time*. The concept behind it becomes crystal-clear in a couple of moves time.

35 ♕c5 ♔g6!! 36 h4 ♖h8!

Now we see the beautiful logic behind Hodgson's play: Black's rook suddenly becomes alive via the h-file. Given Black's artistic king manoeuvre, this example could easily have found itself in Chapter 5.

37 a3 ♖h5 38 ♕g1 ♔h7?!

It's psychologically interesting that despite Hodgson's audacity in moving the king to g6 in order to allow the rook back into the game, he actually now makes a slip by trying to safeguard his king. In fact the king is safer on g6, and 38...♔h7?! only gives White chances to complicate matters. After the absolutely consistent 38...♖f5! Black would be in complete control.

39 ♖d1?

White misses his chance. 39 ♕a7 hits two pawns, but following 39...♖f5 40 ♕xa5 ♖f2 Black's activity is more important than the pawn. However, 39 g4! (I failed to spot this earlier) 39...♖xh4 40 ♕f2! would have secured White some undeserved counterplay, since 40...♖xg4? 41 ♕h2+ ♔g6 42 ♖h1! is very dangerous for Black.

39...♕b3 40 ♖d2 ♖f5!

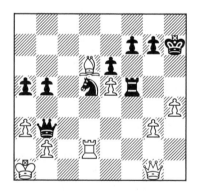

Now Black has everything under command. Just look at the activity of the black rook compared to what it was a few moves ago! The rest of the game is worth seeing if only because it contains a quite stunning finale.

41 g4 ♖f4 42 ♕b1+ ♔g8 43 g5 b4! 44 ♖d3 ♘c3! 45 ♗xb4!

The best move for two reasons. Firstly, it gives Black the chance to blow things with 45...axb4?? 46 ♖d8 mate. Secondly, it allows a wonderful finish. Alternatively, 45 bxc3 loses more prosaically to 45...♕xa3+ 46 ♕a2 ♖f1+.

45...♕a2+!! 0-1

It's mate after 46 ♕xa2 ♖f1+ 47 ♕b1 ♖xb1.

Power Plays

In *Simple Chess* I looked at various examples of the long-term exploitation of an opponent's piece that is permanently placed on a poor square. This theme is most likely to be relevant in closed positions where it may be difficult for one or both sides to manoeuvre freely. However, in more open positions, as in the previous section, it's less likely that a poorly placed piece has no option but to remain where it is. On many occasions a player will use an awkward square as a stepping stone to greener pastures (as in Tseshkovsky-Romanishin above). This idea is seen with all pieces but is particularly relevant to knights. It's certainly not uncommon to see manoeuvres such as ♘b1-a3-c4 (...♘b8-a6-c5), or ♘b1-a3-b5 (...♘b8-a6-b4) – here it's a3 and a6 that

are the 'transition' squares. Very often the plan of using such squares is perfectly okay. However, sometimes, for very few moves, the piece in question is out of play. One player is, in effect, playing with an extra piece for a short while – a kind of *power play*. It goes without saying that this short-term advantage must be exploited quickly and dynamically; pedestrian play will only allow the suffering piece back into the game with no penalty.

I found the following game an excellent example of one player utilising a power play to the full.

Kasparov-Ponomariov
Linares 2003
Queen's Indian Defence

1 ♘f3 ♘f6 2 d4 e6 3 g3 b6 4 ♗g2 ♗b7 5 c4 ♗e7 6 ♘c3 ♘e4 7 ♗d2 ♗f6 8 0-0 0-0 9 ♖c1 d5 10 cxd5 exd5 11 ♗f4 ♘xc3 12 bxc3

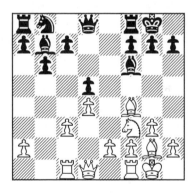

It's true that White has already achieved an edge from the opening, but it's only after Black's next move that his troubles really begin.

12...♘a6?

What prompts such a world-class

grandmaster to make a move like this? Obviously Ponomariov was well aware that the knight stands badly on a6, and I'm pretty sure his plan was to introduce the knight into battle via ...c7-c5 (or ...c7-c6) and ...Nc7-e6. Indeed, if Black could arrange this before White has a chance to achieve anything devastating then he would stand well. However, what Ponomariov overlooked (or perhaps underestimated) was the urgency of Kasparov's response. He exploits the situation of the power play to the full and Black just doesn't get a minute's peace to carry out his plan. What adds to Black's woes is that, as well as being ineffective, the a6-knight is incredibly vulnerable to attack.

Both the other knight moves are superior, although I feel that White still keeps an edge after 12...Nd7 13 Nd2 c5 14 Nc4 (or 14 e4!?) or Kasparov's suggestion of 12...Nc6!? 13 Nd2 Na5! 14 e4 dxe4 15 Nxe4. In the latter variation the black knight also ends up on the edge of the board, but I believe that this is one example of where that old generalisation 'knights on the rim are grim' (or dim, depending on your chess coach) falls down. Although the a5-square is right next to a6, in reality they are worlds apart. On a5 the knight is actually quite well placed; it's protected by a pawn (an outpost!), covers the bishop on b7 and the slight weakness on c6, and also eyes the appealing c4-square. Indeed, the move ...Na5 (or Na4 with colours reversed) is a typical idea against a structure of a-, c- and d-pawns. The Petroff Defence offers many examples of this; for instance, 1 e4 e5 2 Nf3 Nf6 3 Nxe5 d6 4 Nf3 Nxe4 5 d4 d5 6 Bd3 Nc6 7

0-0 Be7 8 c4 Nb4 9 Be2 0-0 10 Nc3 Be6 11 a3 Nxc3 12 bxc3 Nc6 13 cxd5 Bxd5 14 Nd2 Na5! 15 Bd3 b6 (Leko-Kramnik, Dortmund 1999). Another well-known case is the Scotch Four Knights: 1 e4 e5 2 Nf3 Nc6 3 Nc3 Nf6 4 d4 exd4 5 Nxd4 Bb4 6 Nxc6 bxc6 7 Bd3 d5 8 exd5 cxd5 9 0-0 0-0 10 Bg5 c6 and now I like the often-played 11 Na4!, intending ideas such as c2-c4, or c2-c3 with b2-b4.

13 e4!

I find it particularly instructive how Kasparov immediately opens the position to his advantage. Kasparov's second, Yury Dokhoian, sums up the situation perfectly: 'The proposed arena for White's actions is the centre and the kingside, and from a6 the knight will take too long to reach there in time.'

13 c4?! looks inferior. After 13...dxc4 14 Rxc4 c5! the knight on a6 is allowed to show some influence.

13...dxe4 14 Nd2 g5

If White were allowed simply to recapture on e4, then there would be absolutely no disputing his advantage; for example, 14...c5 15 Nxe4 and now 15...Be7 is met by 16 Nf6+!. However, it says something about Black's predicament when the only way forward is to make a weakening lunge on the kingside.

The only other serious option in my view was 14...Re8 15 Re1 and only now 15...g5, but I suspect that this also favours White after 16 Nxe4! Bxe4 17 Bxe4, for example:

a) 17...gxf4 18 Qa4! Rb8 19 Qxa6 (Kasparov) with an obvious advantage to White.

b) 17...Rxe4 18 Rxe4 gxf4 19 Qa4! Qc8 (or 19...Qd5 20 Rce1 Nb8 – what else? – 21 c4 ♕d6 22 ♕e8+ ♔g7 23 ♖xf4 and Black is in a terrible bind) 20 ♖ce1 ♕b7 21 ♖xf4 and the a6-knight is still very far from the action. One possible continuation is 21...♔g7 22 ♕d7 ♕c8 23 ♖g4+ ♔f8 24 ♕d5! ♕xg4 25 ♕xa8+ ♔g7 26 ♕b7 and the knight's fate is sealed.

15 ♗e3!

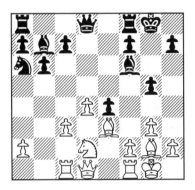

Characteristically, Kasparov opts for the line that leads to a direct attack, and I'm sure that this is the correct decision. 15 ♘xe4 leads to an undisputed advantage for White following 15...♗xe4 16 ♗xe4 gxf4 17 ♕h5 ♖e8 18 ♕xh7+ ♔f8 19 ♗b7! c5 20 ♗xa6 cxd4 21 ♖fd1 (Kasparov), but it seems a shame to relieve Black of that miserable knight.

15...♖e8

Or 15...♕e7 16 ♕h5 c5 17 ♖ce1! (simply massing forces on the kingside) 17...cxd4 18 ♘xe4! dxe3 19 ♘xf6+ ♕xf6 20 ♗xb7 and White wins (Kasparov).

16 f4!

The time is ripe to open more lines.

16...exf3

No better is 16...gxf4 17 ♕g4+ ♔h8 18 ♕xf4.

17 ♗xf3 ♗d5 18 ♗xd5 ♕xd5 19 ♖xf6 ♖xe3 20 ♕g4 20...♖e6 21 ♖f5

♕c6 22 ♕xg5+ ♖g6 23 ♕h5 ♖f8 24 ♘f3 f6 25 ♘h4 ♖g7 26 ♕h6

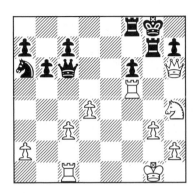

26...♘b8

I find this move quite revealing. Such has been Kasparov's relentless pressure, it's only now, 14 moves after playing ...♘a6, that Ponomariov finds time to relocate the redundant knight, and this is only back to its home square!

27 ♖h5 f5

Black would like to play 27...♘d7, but then 28 ♘f5 ♖gf7 29 ♖g5+! ♔h8 30 ♖g7 (Kasparov) is mating.

28 ♕f4 ♕e4 29 ♖f1 ♕xf4 30 ♖xf4 ♖g4 31 ♖fxf5

Now it's White who's the pawn ahead and the rest is easy work for Kasparov.

31...♘d7 32 ♖xf8+ ♘xf8 33 ♔f2 ♘d7 34 ♘f5 ♔h8 35 ♔f3 ♖g8 36 ♖h6 ♖f8 37 g4 ♘f6 38 c4 ♔g8 39 ♔f4 ♖f7 40 g5 ♘e8 41 ♔e5 ♖d7 42 ♔e6 ♖f7 43 ♖f6! ♘xf6 1-0

44 exf6 ♖f8 45 ♘h6+ ♔h8 46 ♔e7 is a simple win for White.

What's different about the next example is that there is absolutely nothing wrong with Black's initial plan. However, the problem is that Black implements it incorrectly and White is briefly handed a power play. I'm very impressed with the way the Croatian GM Kozul utilises this.

Kozul-Cebalo
Slovenian Team Ch'ship, Celje 2003
Modern Benoni

1 d4 ♘f6 2 ♘f3 e6 3 c4 c5 4 d5 exd5 5 cxd5 d6 6 ♘c3 g6 7 e4 a6 8 a4 ♗g4 9 ♗e2 ♗xf3 10 ♗xf3 ♘bd7 11 0-0 ♗g7 12 ♗f4 ♕e7 13 ♖e1 0-0 14 ♕d2 ♖fe8 15 a5 ♖ac8 16 ♘a4 h5 17 ♖ac1

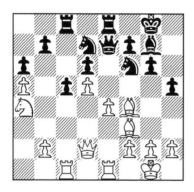

17...♘h7!?

Those of you familiar with this type of position, arising from the Modern Benoni, will appreciate this move. Moving the knight from f6 uncovers the Benoni bishop and increases control over the crucial e5-square. At first sight h7 seems a second-rate square for the knight, but in reality Black is planning ...♗f6 followed by ...♘g5!, when the knight suddenly exerts uncomfortable pressure both on f3 and e4.

18 h3

Prophylaxis against the possible idea of ...g5-g4.

18...♗f6 19 b4!

What particularly appeals to me about

Kozul's play in this game is the way he systematically attacks Black's pawn chain. Attacking the base with e4-e5 is currently out of the question, so White opts to attack the front. Black now has an awkward decision to make: if he captures on b4 then both pawns on d6 and b7 will become vulnerable, but allowing White to capture on c5 will weaken Black's control over the crucial e5-square.

19...♗g5?

Perhaps fearing pressure against d6, Black offers to exchange dark-squared bishops before activating the knight with ...♘g5. However, Kozul's dynamic approach shows that Black's play is faulty, and indeed the knight never actually reaches its intended destination!

In my opinion Black should have continued with the consistent 19...♘g5!. After 20 bxc5 ♘xf3+ 21 gxf3 dxc5 it's true that White has strong central pawns, but for the moment they are held back and Black can certainly seek counterplay against White's weakened kingside structure.

20 bxc5 dxc5

Or 20...♘xc5 21 ♘xc5 ♖xc5 22 ♖xc5 dxc5 23 e5 and White's centre rolls forward, unleashing the power of the f3-bishop.

21 ♘b6!

A logical exchange – White eliminates another defender of the e5-square.

21...♘xb6 22 axb6 ♗xf4 23 ♕xf4 ♕e5

Otherwise White will simply squash Black in the centre with e4-e5.

24 ♕xe5 ♖xe5 25 g3!

The situation is becoming less and less appetising to Black. Unfortunately there is still no time to re-introduce the knight into the game: both 25...♘g5? and 25...♘f6 are met by 26 ♗g2 with the straightforward but extremely strong plan of f2-f4 and e4-e5.

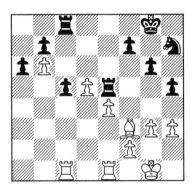

25...f5

A desperate attempt to break up White's centre but, as one would expect, the bishop very much benefits from the opening of the position.

26 d6! ♖d8

26...♘g5 27 ♗g2! fxe4 fails to 28 f4!.

27 exf5

Suddenly the b6-pawn is a big player, and Black simply cannot get his h7-knight back into the game quickly enough.

27...♖xe1+ 28 ♖xe1 ♖xd6 29 ♖e6!
1-0

Offering the exchange of rooks emphasises the hopeless plight of Black's knight. Black resigned here due to variations such as 29...♖xe6 30 fxe6 ♔f8 31 ♗xb7 ♔e7 32 ♗xa6 ♔d6 33 e7 ♘f6 34 ♗b5, and 29...♖d7 30 fxg6 ♘f8 31 ♖e5 ♘xg6 32 ♖g5 ♔g7 33 ♖xc5.

Inducement

In chess tactics and combinations, a *decoy* occurs when a piece lures an enemy one onto a specific line or square that proves to be disadvantageous to the opponent. But of course the same theme can also apply (albeit in a less devastating way) in strategic positions, although here I would prefer to use the word *inducement*. The examples that I find particularly interesting are those where one player actually expends a whole tempo to achieve this goal, the motivation being that the opponent's extra tempo is actually harmful to him. This concept is very common in practical play, but it has often been ignored in chess literature.

The following is an idea that is being witnessed more and more often in several lines of the Sicilian Defence.

1 e4 c5 2 ♘f3 e6 3 d4 cxd4 4 ♘xd4 a6 5 ♘c3 ♕c7 6 ♗d3 ♘f6 7 0-0

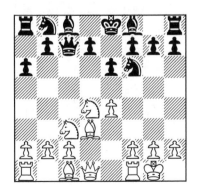

Now a typical plan for Black is to adopt the Scheveningen structure and develop with ...♗e7, ...d7-d6, ...0-0 etc. However, on the way to achieving this set-up it has more recently been fashionable to throw in the move

7...♗c5!

Now it looks as if White can gain time with 8 ♘b3, but after 8...♗e7, followed by ...d6, what has White achieved from this 'extra' tempo? Most Sicilian experts agree that typically the knight stands better on d4 than b3 – its activity more than compensating for its slight vulnerability. There are numerous other Sicilian variations where Black adopts this idea of 'losing' a tempo with an early attack on the d4-knight; for example, 1 e4 c5 2 ♘f3 e6 3 d4 cxd4 4 ♘xd4 a6 5 ♘c3 b5 6 ♗d3 ♕b6!? 7 ♘b3 ♕c7 and 1 e4 c5 2 ♘f3 ♘c6 3 d4 cxd4 4 ♘xd4 ♕b6 5 ♘b3 ♘f6 6 ♘c3 e6 7 ♗e3 ♕c7.

Here's a slightly more complex example taken from the common opening sequence

1 d4 ♘f6 2 c4 e6 3 ♘f3 b6 4 g3 ♗a6 5 b3

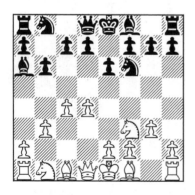

I admit that Black has quite a few ways to proceed here, but the most common plan these days is to obtain a solid grip on the centre with ...c7-c6 and ...d7-d5. If White reacts to this idea by simply exchanging on d5 then the point is to recapture with the c-pawn, leaving Black with a rock-solid formation and an active bishop on a6 against a rather passive one on g2. So, all in all, it certainly makes sense for White to avoid this exchange if possible.

Let's play a few natural moves:

5...c6 6 ♗g2 d5 7 0-0 ♘bd7

The immediate 7...dxc4?! can be met favourably by 8 ♘e5!.

8 ♘bd2! ♗e7 9 ♗b2 0-0

All normal stuff. White has easily solved the problem of the attacked c4-pawn, his pieces are in natural positions and he can claim an edge.

Now let's see what happens if Black's approach is a little more subtle:

5...♗b4+!

Inducing White's next move.

6 ♗d2

For reasons given below, this bishop is less favourably placed on d2 than on c1, but White really had no choice. 6 ♘fd2? is obviously ridiculous and leaves White somewhat embarrassed after 6...♗b7!. The move 6 ♘bd2? seemingly makes more sense but in fact leads White into surprising trouble. I can't resist quoting the game Shirazi-Benjamin, Berkeley 1984, if nothing else because I can't recall an international master playing White getting into such a farcical tangle after so few moves: 6...♗c3! 7 ♖b1 ♗b7! (threatening ...♗e4) 8 ♗b2 ♘e4! 9 ♖g1? ♕f6! 10 ♗c1 (what else?) 10...♘c6 11 e3 ♘b4 and White can already resign (instead he chose to play on with the humorous 12 ♖b2?!!).

6...♗e7 7 ♗g2

I don't wish to lunge into a theoretical discussion of this line of the Queen's Indian. It's sufficient to say that White has other options here and over the next few moves. But let's try to play as in the example above with 5...c6.

7...c6 8 0-0 d5

Now White must begin thinking about his c-pawn. For the moment there is no problem (9...dxc4 can be answered by 10 ♘e5), but Black will play ...♘bd7 next move, after which the threat will become real. To reach the same set-up as above, White needs to remove his bishop from d2 so that the b1-knight can take this square.

9 ♗c3 ♘bd7 10 ♘bd2 0-0

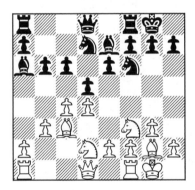

We have reached exactly the same position as the example above except for the fact that White's dark-squared bishop has been lured to c3 (rather than its normal home at b2). This may seem like an insignificant point, but it's nuances like this that can change an assessment from an edge to White to equality. The bishop is undoubtedly slightly worse on c3: it hinders any White action on the c-file and is more vulnerable to attack, either along the c-file or, if White captures

on d5, with ...♘xd5.

Without going into detail, the move 11 ♖e1, intending e2-e4, is White's most popular choice here. However, it's revealing to note that I found numerous examples of White admitting a loss of time by playing 11 ♗b2!?.

Below is an example of inducement that especially attracted me. It's slightly different from the previous two in that here a certain piece (that poor knight again; I'm afraid its having a rough time in this chapter!) is made redundant after a pawn is lured to a fateful square, thus blocking its path into the game.

Vydeslaver-Fressinet
European Club Cup, Rethymnon 2003
Sicilian Defence

1 e4 c5 2 ♘f3 ♘c6 3 ♗b5 g6 4 0-0 ♗g7 5 c3 ♘f6 6 e5 ♘d5 7 d4 cxd4 8 ♗xc6 dxc6 9 ♕xd4 ♗f5 10 ♘a3 h6 11 h3 g5 12 ♖e1 ♘b6 13 h4 g4 14 ♕f4 gxf3 15 ♕xf5 fxg2 16 ♕g4 ♔f8 17 e6!

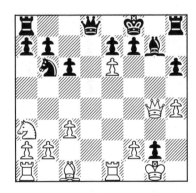

In a rather messy position White has just played the move 17 e6!, logically looking to open lines against Black's king in the centre. What I especially enjoy about this game is the fact that the Laurent Fressinet seems to be under the cosh for a period of time, but always lurking in the background is the fact that White is essentially playing the position a piece down. At first, when White is pursuing the initiative, this doesn't seem to matter too much, but as the game progresses the missing piece becomes more and more relevant.

17...♕d5!

A strong centralised square for Black's queen, which can influence both defence and attack. It's unsurprising that White is in a hurry to banish the queen from d5, but this is exactly what Black wants!

18 c4

When annotating this game, Fressinet revealed: 'I was very pleased to see this move as I knew that the white knight would find it hard to join the attack. In fact the pawn takes away the knight's square.'

18...♕d3!

The logical follow-up to Black's previous move. The queen is kept centralised and prevents White from playing ♘c2. Note that the fateful move c3-c4 has also increased the scope of the g7-bishop, which now powers down to b2. As a direct consequence it's difficult for White to develop the c1-bishop quickly.

19 exf7 ♘d7!

A familiar theme: Black improves his worst placed piece. Crucially, it is easier for Black to do this than it is for White. Now 20 ♖d1 can be answered by 20...♘e5! 21 ♖xd3 ♘xg4.

20 ♗f4 ♘f6 21 ♕e6 ♕d7 22 ♕e3?

Perhaps White was under the illusion that his attack on the kingside was going

to bear fruit, but he was mistaken. In some ways his decision is understandable – it is, after all, difficult to foresee Black's 23rd move. Instead of this misplaced hope, a dose of realism was required. After 22 ♕xd7! ♘xd7 the endgame is roughly level.

22...♔xf7 23 ♖ad1 ♕f5!

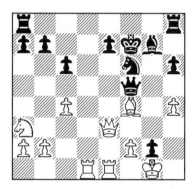

A star move and very cool play from the French GM. At first sight it looks like it's inviting real trouble by allowing White to capture on e7, but in fact this is not the case.

24 ♕xe7+ ♔g6 25 ♕e3?

The second time in four moves that White plays this unfortunate move.

The direct attack with 25 ♖e3? is repelled comfortably by the continuation 25...♕xf4 26 ♖g3+ ♘g4 27 ♕d6+ ♕xd6 28 ♖xd6+ ♔h5. Instead White should bail out into a worse ending after 25 ♕e5 ♕h3 26 ♗h2 ♖he8 27 ♕g3+ ♕xg3 28 ♗xg3 ♘e4 (Fressinet).

25...♖ae8 26 ♕g3+ ♔h7 27 ♖xe8 ♖xe8

Slowly but surely Black's advantage is becoming more and more apparent, and now there is absolutely no dispute. It's another power play situation and Fressinet takes full advantage.

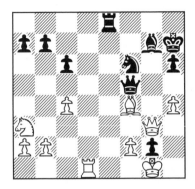

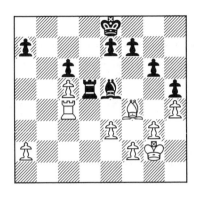

28 ♗e3 ♘e4 29 ♕f4 ♕h3 30 ♕h2 ♕f3 31 ♖d7 ♘f6

31...♘xf2! is even stronger, as 32 ♗xf2 allows 32...♖e1+ 33 ♗xe1 ♕f1 mate.

32 ♖xg7+

Transposing into a hopeless ending, but 32 ♖xb7 would lose to 32...♖xe3!.

32...♔xg7 33 ♕xg2+ ♕xg2+ 34 ♔xg2 a6 35 ♔f3 ♔g6 36 b3 ♖f8 37 ♔e2 ♘g4 38 ♗b6 ♔h5 39 ♘c2 ♔xh4 40 ♘e1 ♖e8+ 0-1

Exercises

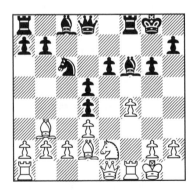

Exercise 1.1: White to Play

Single out which minor piece White would most like to improve. Can you find a clever way to achieve this?

Exercise 1.2: White to play

Black has just retreated his bishop from d4 to e5, offering an exchange. How should White proceed?

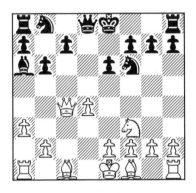

Exercise 1.3: White to play

Black has just played ...♗c8-a6, attacking White's queen. How would you respond?

CHAPTER TWO

Inside Trading

One subject that I only touched upon from time to time in *Simple Chess* but would very much like to delve into here is the technique of exchanging (or trading, if you're the other side of the Atlantic) pieces and pawns. Of course this is an incredibly broad topic and it's no coincidence that this is by far the biggest chapter in the book.

The stronger a chess player becomes, the more important the role of exchanging pieces. Here it's worth quoting three-time world champion Mikhail Botvinnik, who certainly knew a thing or two about, amongst other things, exchanging pieces: 'In my opinion, the process of chess is based essentially on interlinking exchanges. The objective of these interlinking exchanges is a relative gain ... of material or of positional value. There are no other and cannot be any other objectives. At the end of the game these exchanges must lead to a gain of infinitely large magnitude (to mate)'.

Most great players in the history of chess have been particularly skilful in the art of exchanging. Anatoly Karpov and Bobby Fischer, to name two, particularly stand out in this respect. They naturally and instinctively seem to know which pieces need to be exchanged and how to bring the best out of the ones remaining on the board.

In every exchange there is something to be gained and something to be lost for both parties. Having just read over that previous sentence again I do realise that I could be accused of, as Basil Fawlty would say, 'stating the bleeding obvious'. But you know what I mean – I'm talking about a gain or loss of time, a change in structure, control over a square, an opening of a line or diagonal etc.

In his excellent and thought-provoking 'Strategy' column for *Chess-Base Magazine*, grandmaster Peter Wells very helpfully categorises the important questions that you should ask yourself every time a reduction of material is imminent. I hope he won't mind me repeating, expanding and elaborating on them here:

1) What are the relative strengths and weaknesses of the candidate pieces to be exchanged?

2) What structural changes may arise directly as a result of the exchange?

3) In addition to the decision 'to exchange or not' is there a further issue of either carrying out the exchange or merely permitting it to consider? In many scenarios there are three options: to actively exchange, to permit an exchange or to actively avoid an exchange.

4) Will the exchange have an impact upon the relative strengths and weaknesses of the other pieces that remain on the board?

5) Is the piece that might be exchanged in fact performing a function in a concrete situation that a static/rule-based assessment would tend to overlook? A piece may be 'bad' in the traditional sense or look rather clumsy, but it could still be the very same piece that holds a position together.

6) Will the exchange open new avenues of attack (or defence) for either player?

7) Will the exchange speed up the development for either player?

What I've attempted to do in this chapter, as much as possible, is to isolate and thus highlight all the many important reasons for exchanging a piece, simply permitting an exchange or actively avoiding an exchange. In this way I hope that the reader can benefit from this by identifying the aspects to look for when trading material. Inevitably in some examples there's more than one thing to look out for; that is, a player may well have more than one reason to carry out or avoid an exchange. In general, though, there will be one overriding factor in each decision.

I should say that I'm more interested in cases where it's obvious that there are both pros and cons to seeking or avoiding an exchange and this is reflected in the majority of the examples that I've chosen. It wouldn't be helpful to fill these pages with too many lopsided examples in which only one player gains from the exchange. Mastering the technique of exchanging comes with practice of adding up what is gained and what is given up in a trade, and assessing the importance of these. Some of the decisions taken by the players in these examples are outwardly surprising, and these judgements can only be understood after a deep appraisal of the positions.

In the main I have concentrated here on trading pieces of equal traditional values (rook for rook, bishop for bishop, bishop for knight etc.). On occasions, however, I have strayed into the territory of what you could term as 'unlike exchanges', but these are more commonly known as positional sacrifices (see page 36 for more on this).

I haven't specifically concentrated on the similar subject of 'trading advantages' (material for positional or one type of positional for another), but there are a few examples in which this concept is clearly seen.

Early impressions of exchanges

Like most chess players, my earliest memories of exchanges were that they proved to be very good tools for exploiting material advantages. The simple rule was that in a position of material advantage it was a good idea to swap pieces (but not too many pawns). See the simplified example below:

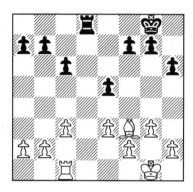

In this position White obviously has many roads to victory, but most would agree that the easiest way to exploit the substantial material plus is with **1 ♖d1!**. Then Black is in a no-win situation: he either has to exchange rooks, leaving White with an easier technical task then before, or he must give up control of the d-file and allow White's rook to infiltrate the seventh rank via d7. From there the rook will create havoc.

The only thing White has to be careful of in a situation like this is not to exchange too many pawns. In an extreme case, if all the pawns were exchanged, White would be left with rook and bishop versus rook – a standard theoretical draw.

I should say that this rule of exchanging pieces to exploit material advantage is very often misused (in a similar way weaker players often mistakenly think that the easiest way to draw with a stronger player is to exchange pieces at every opportunity, regardless of the positional consequences). In the following game I was guilty of exchanging a pair of pieces simply for the sake of exchange and I was punished accordingly.

Emms-Summerscale
Hastings 1997/98

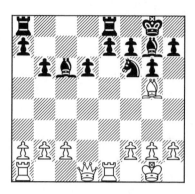

Having won a queen for bishop, knight and pawn with a neat trick in the early middlegame, I now made a big mistake of writing this position off as an easy win, and my remarkable casualness was demonstrated in my very poor choice of a couple of moves.

17 c3?!

Inaccurate, but not a disaster. Nevertheless, 17 f3, blunting the c6-bishop and preventing any ideas of ...♘e4, was stronger, and after 17...h6 18 ♗e3! ♘d5 19 ♗d4 e5 20 ♗f2 White should eventually be able to convert his material advantage.

17...h6 18 ♗xf6?

This piece of exchanging for the sake of it is criminal. I made the fatal beginner-like error of not examining the actual pros and cons of the exchange, simply believing that all 'similar' exchanges would lead to victory.

18 ♗d2 ♘e4 19 ♗e3 is only a slightly inferior version of the note to White's 17th move.

18...♗xf6

Gradually over the next few moves it dawned on me that my superficial exchanging had simply left a position in which I could make no progress whatsoever. Black has no weaknesses and the bishop pair dominates. For a while I was even a little worried that Black could make progress (now that would have been a real punishment!). In the end we shuffled around for a twenty-odd moves before I sheepishly offered a draw.

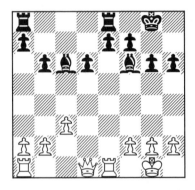

19 ♕d3 ♖ad8 20 a4 ♖d7 21 a5 b5 22 ♖ad1 ♔g7 23 h3 ♖b8 24 ♖d2 ♖c7 25 ♖c2 ♗d7 26 ♖ce2 ♗c6 27 ♕d2 ♖d8 28 ♕d1 ♖b8 29 ♕d2 ♖bc8 30 ♕d3 ♔f8 31 ♕e3 ♔g7 32 ♕g3 ♗a8 33 ♕d3 a6 34 ♖e3 ♖d7 35 ♖3e2 ♖c5 36 ♖e3 ♖dc7 37 ♕d2 ♗b7 38 ♕d3 ♖d5 39 ♕e2 ♖g5 40 f3 ♖gc5 41 ♖d3 ♗a8 42 ♖ed1 ½-½

An exchange as part of a combination

Before moving onto more complex issues, I think it's worth mentioning another normal role for the exchange, that of being a basic element in a combination. Here is a typical example, taken from one of my own games.

Emms-Benito
Benidorm 1991

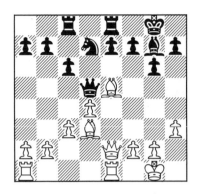

White wins with a straightforward combination:

17 ♗c4! ♕a5

The only move.

18 ♗xg7!

This exchange is a vital element of the combination.

18...♔xg7 19 ♗xf7!

Winning a pawn due to 19...♔xf7 20 ♕e6+ ♔g7 21 ♕xd7. The game ended:
20 ♗e6 ♖c7 21 ♕e3 ♖f6 22 b4 ♕h5? 23 ♕g3! 1-0

Here's a more recent example, taken from a higher level.

Adams-Bareev
Wijk aan Zee 2004

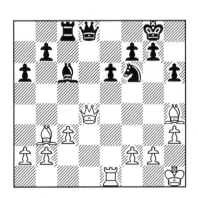

23 ♗xf6! ♕xf6?

Though it is obviously undesirable to weaken the kingside with the queens still remaining on the board, Black must play 23...gxf6.

24 ♕xf6! gxf6 25 ♖xe6!

The combinational follow-up to the exchanges. Black loses a vital pawn and in fact here Bareev chose to resign immediately.

Removing a defender

An exchange can be a major weapon for removing an opponent's defending piece. Often this type of exchange is a vital component of a successful attack against an opposing king.

Vukcevich-Van Hoorne
World Student Team Ch'ship,
Leningrad 1960

This position has arisen from the main line of the Dragon Sicilian, in which players castle on opposite sides and launch direct attacks on the opposing kings. Often these assaults include many sacrifices, but this doesn't always have to be the case.

The black knight on f6 is an absolutely vital defender, so what should White do?

21 ♘d5!

Exactly! There's no need for fireworks when a simple exchange will do.

21...♘xd5 22 ♕h7+

Okay, I wasn't being completely honest in my last comment. White doesn't even bother to recapture on d5 when there are bigger fish to fry. That said, the slower 22 exd5 is also good enough, as there is no really good defence to ♕h7+ followed by ♗h6; for example, 22...♔f8 23 ♕h7 e5 24 ♗h6 ♗xh6 25 ♕xh6+ ♔e7 26 ♕h4+ f6 27 ♕h7+ ♔d8 28 ♕g8+ ♗e8 29 ♖h8 ♖e7 30 ♘c6+ and White wins.

22...♔f8

Now the bishop on g7 is Black's only real defender, so...

23 ♗h6!

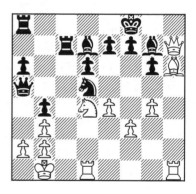

Now 23...♗xh6 24 ♕h8 is mate. Black can already resign.

23...♘c3+ 24 bxc3 e6 25 ♕xg7+ ♔e7 26 ♘f5+! exf5 27 ♗g5+ 1-0

The previous case was tactical in nature and reasonably straightforward. It's true to say that when you are going for mate, you're not really too bothered by the positional intricacies of an exchange. In general, though, I'm more interested in looking at removing defenders in a more long-term and strategic sense. An opposing piece can still be a useful defender even if it is protecting an important square rather than the king, as in the following example.

Bologan-M.Gurevich
France 1994
French Defence

1 e4 e6 2 d4 d5 3 ♘c3 ♘f6 4 e5 ♘fd7 5 ♘ce2 c5 6 c3 ♘c6 7 ♘f3 cxd4 8 cxd4 f6 9 ♘f4 ♗b4+ 10 ♗d2 ♕e7 11 ♗xb4 ♕xb4+ 12 ♕d2 ♕xd2+ 13 ♔xd2 ♔e7 14 exf6+ ♘xf6

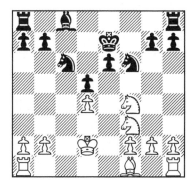

I believe that in this position the black knight on c6 is a good piece. My reasoning is that it simply covers the hole (or outpost, depending from which side you are looking) on e5. Of course White would love to be able to plonk a knight on that square without giving Black the option of capturing it.

What's the solution to White's problem? Exchange the light-squared bishop for the c6-knight! Of course in this position the f1-bishop is traditionally 'good' (the d4-pawn is on a dark square), but

here this fact is irrelevant in the overall picture. Domination of e5 is the key.

15 ♗b5! ♘e4+ 16 ♔e3 ♖f8?!

16...♗d7 17 ♗xc6 ♗xc6 18 ♘e5 (Bologan) is more resilient, but still good for White.

17 ♗xc6! bxc6 18 ♖hc1 ♗d7 19 ♘d3 ♖ab8 20 ♘fe5

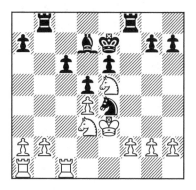

After a few preparatory moves, White finally sinks a knight into the e5 outpost. Black's only possible way of challenging this piece is with the knight on e4, but even in this event (as in the game) there is another one on d3 waiting to take its place. It's instructive to see how easily Black's position crumbles in the face of a good knight versus bad bishop scenario.

20...♖b6 21 ♖c2 a5 22 ♖ac1 ♖c8 23 g4 ♗e8 24 f3 ♘d6 25 h4 ♘f7 26 ♖c5! ♘xe5 27 ♘xe5 ♖xb2 28 ♖xa5 ♖b7 29 ♖a6 ♔d6 30 ♘d3 ♖bb8 31 ♖c3 ♖c7 32 ♖ca3 ♗g6 33 ♘e5 ♗e8 34 ♖a7 ♖bc8 35 ♖xc7 ♖xc7 36 ♖a8 ♔e7 37 ♘d3 ♖b7 38 ♘c5 ♖b1 39 ♖a7+ ♔d6 40 ♖xg7

and Bologan comfortably won the endgame.

Experienced readers may well have seen this following example before, but I make no apologies for including it. It's by this famous exchange that all other exchanges are judged.

Fischer-Petrosian
7th match game, Buenos Aires 1971

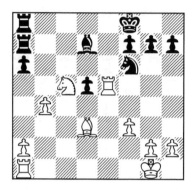

Let's first of all view things from a conventional standpoint. White has an excellent knight – it's securely placed on an outpost in the heart of Black's position. At the same time, Black's bishop on d7 is 'bad' – it's obstructed by the central pawn on d5. This is what made Fischer's next move so perplexing at the time it was played.

22 ♘xd7+!

In the entertaining book *Learn from the Grandmasters*, American GM Yasser Seirawan chooses this game as one of his favourites of all time. He describes it as a 'total crush' and relates in his own words how GM Robert Byrne, columnist for the *New York Times*, told him the following story about what was going on in the press room at the time of 22 ♘xd7: 'R.Byrne continues: This brought the house down! GM Miguel Najdorf jumped up and started shouting, "My God!! He's crazy!! Such a knight!! My God!! How can he give up such a knight

for such a terrible bishop?" Of course no one understood Bobby the way I did ... According to the way he played chess, Bobby was just driving the nails into the coffin. The bishop may look bad but it's not. The position is open. The c5-knight is great but it blocks the open c-file. Finally, the d3-bishop is so much superior to the knight when there are pawns on both sides of the board. Bobby was just using his principles.'

There's not much more that I need to add to that! Except perhaps it should be said that, despite being traditionally bad, the d7-bishop is actually a very useful defensive piece here because it covers possible infiltration points (including the c6-square) and also prepares to challenge the d3-bishop with ...♗b5. It's true that White can prevent this with a2-a4, but then Black can fall back on the idea of ...♗c6 and ...♘d7, challenging that knight on c5. I guess this example would fall under category '5' in the introduction: the more you look at it, the more it's that bishop that holds Black's position together. Offhand I can't recall who, but I think that someone famous once said that the worst bishop is stronger than the best knight. I guess that this would be an example to back up a rather extreme statement.

This example could also easily be viewed from different perspectives. You could say White is merely trading positional advantages, or simply considering the strength of the remaining pieces (see page 57), or, as GM Mihai Suba would say, getting rid of the 'impurities' in the position.

22...♖xd7 23 ♖c1 ♖d6

A concession that comes directly from

22 ♘xd7 – White was threatening to penetrate with ♖c6.

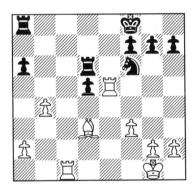

24 ♖c7 ♘d7 25 ♖e2 g6 26 ♔f2 h5 27 f4 h4 28 ♔f3 f5 29 ♔e3 d4+ 30 ♔d2 ♘b6 31 ♖ee7

I wonder if anyone in the pressroom was arguing with Fischer's earlier decision now.

31...♘d5 32 ♖f7+ ♔e8 33 ♖b7 ♘xb4 34 ♗c4 1-0

Here Petrosian resigned in view of White's unstoppable threat of 35 ♖h7 ♖f6 36 ♖h8+ ♖f8 37 ♗f7+ ♔d8 38 ♖xf8 mate.

The following is a fragment that illustrates all too well the problems of losing an effective defender.

Milov-Luther
Merida 2003
Slav Defence

1 d4 d5 2 c4 c6 3 ♘f3 ♘f6 4 e3 a6 5 ♗d3 ♗g4 6 ♕b3 ♗xf3 7 gxf3 ♖a7 8 ♘c3 e6 9 c5 ♘bd7 10 ♗d2 e5 11 ♕c2 g6 12 f4 exd4 13 exd4

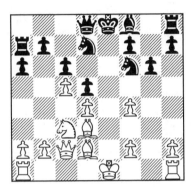

White's plan is to castle queenside and launch a pawn offensive on the other wing. Nevertheless, after 13...♗g7 followed by ...0-0 Black would be fairly well protected on that side of the board and could look to the future with some confidence. Instead there came:

13...♗h6?

The seemingly ambitious move is seriously flawed, and I like the way Milov refutes it with direct play.

14 0-0-0 0-0 15 f5!

Naturally! Black can now only keep this excellent defensive bishop by admitting his mistake and giving up a full tempo with the embarrassing retreat 15...♗g7. Instead Black ploughed on and the game continued...

15...♗xd2+ 16 ♕xd2 ♘h5 17 ♖hg1

...and unsurprisingly White's automatic attack on the kingside was ultimately successful.

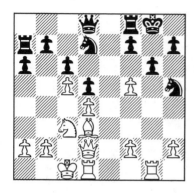

Removing an attacker

Just as it can be vital to remove defending pieces, it can be just as important to exchange an opponent's attacking piece. Perhaps I should actually use the word 'active' rather than 'attacking': the piece in question can be active but doesn't necessarily have to be attacking the king.

Spassky-Petrosian

World Ch'ship (Game 1), Moscow 1969
Sicilian Defence

1 e4 c5 2 ♘f3 e6 3 d4 cxd4 4 ♘xd4 a6 5 ♗d3 ♘c6 6 ♘xc6 bxc6 7 0-0 d5 8 ♘d2 ♘f6 9 ♕e2 ♗e7 10 b3 0-0 11 ♗b2 a5 12 f4 g6 13 ♖ad1 ♘d7 14 c4 a4 15 f5 exf5 16 exf5

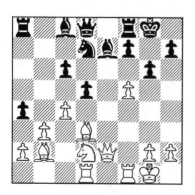

White's set-up on the kingside looks threatening, but I'm impressed by the way Petrosian coolly defuses the situation.

16...♗f6!

Simply offering to exchange one of White's most effective attacking pieces for a piece that was doing little on e7. White can hardly refuse this swap.

17 ♗xf6

17 fxg6? doesn't work: 17...♗xb2 18 gxf7+ ♖xf7 19 ♖xf7 ♔xf7 20 ♕h5+ ♔f8 21 ♖f1+ ♘f6 22 ♕xh7 ♕e7 and Black rebuffs the attack.

17...♘xf6 18 ♕f2 axb3 19 axb3 ♖a2!? 20 fxg6?!

This move releases the tension too quickly and allows Black to use the f-file as well as White. Geller gave 20 ♗b1 ♖a5 21 ♕h4 as an improvement, but 21...♔g7! 22 b4 ♖a3 looks okay for Black, who may follow up with ...♘h5. Note that Black's king is happy on a dark square now that there is no bishop on b2 to worry about.

20...fxg6 21 h3 ♕e7

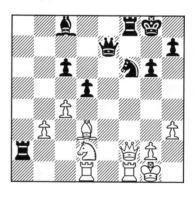

and Black has a fully acceptable position. The rest of the game is of no relevance to our theme, Petrosian winning after more errors from Spassky.

Next we see Vishy Anand give a demonstration of high-class trading.

Illescas Cordoba-Anand
Linares 1994
Caro-Kann Defence

1 e4 c6 2 d4 d5 3 exd5 cxd5 4 ♗d3 ♘c6 5 c3 ♕c7 6 ♗g5 ♘f6 7 ♘d2 ♗g4 8 ♘gf3 e6 9 ♗h4 ♗d6 10 ♗g3

10...♗h5!
Preparing to oppose White's strongest minor piece with ...♗g6.
11 ♗xd6 ♕xd6 12 0-0 0-0 13 ♖e1 ♖ab8 14 a4 ♕c7 15 ♕b1 a6 16 ♘e5 ♖fe8 17 h3 ♗g6!
Now White must part with either his strong knight on e5 or the bishop on d3. Either way, Black's position improves.
18 ♗xg6
Anand gives the line 18 ♘xg6 hxg6 19 ♘f3 e5 and assesses this as slightly better for Black. After 20 dxe5 ♘xe5 21 ♕d1 ♘xf3+ 22 ♕xf3 ♕b6 I would be more inclined to suggest that the position is balanced, with White's vulnerable queen-side pawns balancing the typical weakness of the isolated queen's pawn (IQP).
18...hxg6 19 ♕d3 ♘xe5 20 dxe5?!
After this error White begins to strug-

gle. He hasn't enough pieces to arrange an attack on the kingside and his pawn structure is less compact than Black's. 20 ♖xe5! is stronger, after which Anand suggests 20...♖ec8, intending ...♘e8-d6.
20...♘d7 21 ♕d4 ♖ec8 22 ♖e3 ♕b6!

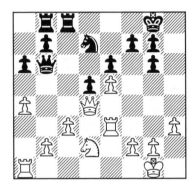

Forcing the queens off — another good trade for Black. In the arising ending White's pawns are vulnerable and Black can make use of the half-open c-file. I suspect that White's position is already difficult, and another mistake on move 26 does not help. In any case it's already clear in this position that Black's exchanges have been very favourable for him.
23 ♕xb6 ♘xb6 24 h4 ♔f8 25 g3 ♔e7 26 b3? ♖c7 27 a5 ♘d7 28 c4 ♖bc8 29 ♔g2 ♘b8! 30 ♖a4 ♖d8! 31 f4 ♘c6 32 ♖d3 ♖cd7 33 c5 f6 34 ♘f3 d4! 35 exf6+ gxf6 36 ♘d2 e5 37 ♘e4 ♖d5! 38 fxe5 ♖xe5 39 ♘d6 ♖xc5 40 ♘xb7? ♖c2+ 0-1
After 41 ♔h3, 41...♖b8 traps the knight.

In this following example, the piece to be exchanged is performing a dual attacking and defensive role.

Lalic-Chandler
Hastings 2000
Catalan Opening

1 d4 ♘f6 2 c4 e6 3 g3 d5 4 ♘f3 dxc4 5 ♗g2 a6 6 0-0 ♘c6 7 ♘c3 ♖b8 8 e4 ♗e7 9 ♕e2 b5 10 ♖d1 ♘b4 11 ♘e5

White's knight on e5 is a very strong piece both in attack (there are certainly possibilities of a2-a3 and then ♘c6) and defence (Black's outpost on d3-square is covered). Chandler solves all his problems with a simple offer of a trade.

11...♘d7!

Chandler rightly judges that the defensive qualities of the f6-knight are less relevant here than the attributes of White's knight on e5 – there is something to be gained from the exchange of these pieces.

11...♗b7 is less effective: 12 a3! ♘d3 (12...♘c6? 13 ♘xc6 ♗xc6 14 d5! exd5 15 e5 ♘d7 16 ♘xd5 is just what White is looking for) 13 ♘xd3 cxd3 14 ♖xd3 gave White a little something in Ivanisevic-Abramovic Yugoslavia 1999.

12 b3

12 ♕g4!? is a more obvious way to try to exploit the absence of a black knight

on f6, but after 12...g6 (but not 12...0-0? 13 ♗h6 ♗f6? 14 ♘xd7 ♗xd7 15 e5) 13 ♗h6 ♘xe5 14 dxe5 ♘d3 Lalic assesses this as slightly better for Black and I agree, despite the fact that castling is not an option at the moment. One possible continuation is 15 ♗f1 b4 16 ♗xd3 cxd3 17 ♘e2 c5 18 b3 ♗b7 19 ♘c1 ♕d4 followed by ...♕xe4.

12...♘xe5

Not falling for the trick 12...cxb3? 13 a3! ♘c2 14 ♘c6 – a smothered mate on Black's queen!

13 dxe5 ♘d3 14 ♗e3 0-0 15 f4 ♗b4 16 ♕c2 ♕e7 17 ♘e2 a5!

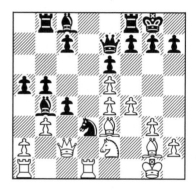

Making room for ...♗a6 to support Black's extra pawn (18 bxc4 bxc4 19 ♕xc4? allows 19...♘b2). Black has a clear advantage here and Chandler went on to win the game.

Exchanging your worst placed piece

Do you realise Fischer almost never has any bad pieces. He exchanges them, and the bad pieces remain with his opponents. – Yuri Balashov

We've already dealt with the worst placed piece to some extent in Chapter 1, where we looked at ways of both exploiting your opponent's and improving your own. It's a sure sign of a class player when he or she never appears to be lumbered with a poorly placed piece. One of the solutions to having a problem piece is simply to exchange it off, as in the following example.

Plachetka-Azmaiparashvili
Stary Smokovec 1983
Pirc Defence

1 d4 d6 2 e4 g6 3 ♘c3 ♗g7 4 ♘f3 ♘f6 5 ♗e2 0-0 6 0-0 ♗g4 7 ♗e3 ♘c6 8 h3 ♗xf3 9 ♗xf3 e5 10 dxe5 dxe5 11 ♘e2 ♕e7 12 c3 ♖fb8 13 b4 a5 14 b5 ♘d8 15 ♕a4 ♘e6 16 ♖fd1

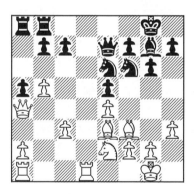

Black's worst placed minor piece is the bishop on g7, traditionally 'bad' due to the pawn on e5. Of course Black could try to activate this piece via the f8-a3 diagonal, but Azmaiparashvili has something more powerful in mind.

16...h5!

With the rather cheeky plan of ...♔h7 and ....♗h6!, trading a bishop that's not pulling its weight for a far more effective one. The trouble from White's point of view is that there is nothing that can be done about this!

17 ♖d2 ♔h7 18 ♖ad1?

Too automatic. White has control of the d-file but this is of little use because Black covers all the points of entry.

Azmaiparashvili suggests improving one of White's own minor pieces with 18 ♘g3, intending to meet ....♗h6 with ♘f1 and recapturing on e3 with the knight.

18...♗h6 19 ♗xh6 ♔xh6 20 ♘c1 ♘g5 21 ♕c4 ♔g7!

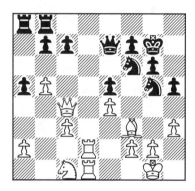

The bishop on f3 is so bad that Black is rightly reluctant to play ...♘xf3, even though this would shatter White's kingside formation. This moves me on to considering something further than simply Black successfully trading off his worst piece. This example could easily have fallen into the category of 'exchanging one bishop of a bishop pair'. Going back to the introduction to this chapter and to question number 4, we ask ourselves: 'Will the exchange have an impact upon the relative strengths and weaknesses of the other pieces that remain on the board?' In this case the answer is most certainly 'Yes!' The bishop on f3 feels very poorly without its partner in crime (see Chapter 3 for more on this).

Yet another possible category could

have been 'exchanging to control a colour complex' (see page 60) – the f3-bishop is the only minor piece remaining which cannot contribute to the control of the dark squares.

22 ♘d3 ♖d8 23 ♘e1 ♖xd2 24 ♖xd2 ♖d8 25 ♖xd8 ♕xd8 26 ♕e2 ♕d7 27 h4 ♘e6 28 ♕d3 ♘c5 29 ♕xd7 ♘fxd7 30 ♘c2 ♘f6

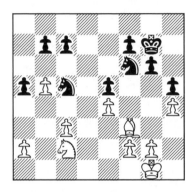

White's troubles continue into the endgame: the bishop on f3 is miserable and White has numerous pawn weaknesses. Azmaiparashvili successfully converts Black's advantages into the full point.

31 ♘e3 ♘fxe4 32 ♘d5 c6 33 bxc6 bxc6 34 ♗xe4 ♘xe4 35 ♘e7 ♘xc3 36 ♘xc6 a4 37 ♘b4 ♔f6 38 ♔f1 ♔f5 39 ♔e1 ♔g4 40 ♔d2 ♘xa2! 41 ♘xa2 ♔xh4 42 ♔c2 e4! 43 ♘c3 e3! 44 fxe3 ♔g3 0-1

There's no stopping the h-pawn.

I was particularly impressed with Black's play in the next example, as the solution to his problems is not the first that springs to mind. Unless you are familiar with this type of position, Mickey Adams's idea takes a bit of getting used to.

Gelfand-Adams
Wijk aan Zee 2002
Ruy Lopez

1 e4 e5 2 ♘f3 ♘c6 3 ♗b5 a6 4 ♗a4 ♘f6 5 0-0 ♗e7 6 ♖e1 b5 7 ♗b3 0-0 8 h3 ♗b7 9 d3 d6 10 a3 ♘a5 11 ♗a2 c5 12 ♘c3 ♘c6 13 ♘e2

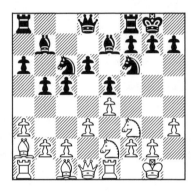

At first sight there is nothing at all wrong with Black's bishop on b7. Indeed, black pawns on c5, d6 and e5 indicate that it's 'good' in the conventional sense. It's true that at the moment it is blocked by the knight on c6, but this is a problem that could easily be rectified by Black: the knight is certainly not stuck on this square. A more serious issue, though, is White's own pawn structure in the centre (c2, d3, e4), which is specifically designed to blunt the power of this bishop. Black does have ways (specifically pawn breaks) to activate the bishop on the b7-square, but these are either difficult to arrange successfully (as in the case of ...f7-f5), or lead to problems in the centre (for example, the immediate 13...d5 14 exd5 ♘xd5 15 ♘g3 ♗f6 16 ♘e4 looks more pleasant for White).

I admit that when talking of 'the worst placed piece', some elasticity is required.

I guess one could argue that the bishop on b7 is really no worse than the one on e7, but the fact is that Black can only do one thing at a time! Besides, there is no real obvious method to improve the e7-bishop at the moment.

13...♗c8!

Once you get over the fact that the bishop is 'undeveloping' itself from a square it only went to a few moves ago, it's easy to appreciate this move. The main point is to play ...♗e6, offering an exchange to the bishop on a2 (I guess that this example could have been placed in the previous section – the bishop on a2 is no mean piece). However, as we see in the resulting play, there's more than one point to ...♗c8.

I should point out that Black can get away with such an 'undeveloping' move here because the position is basically closed so White has no quick way to exploit Black's slow manoeuvring.

14 ♘g3 ♗e6 15 ♘f5?!

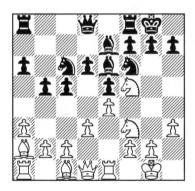

Allowing Black to demonstrate another point of ...♗c8: control of the crucial f5-square.

White should probably be content with 15 ♗xe6 fxe6 16 c3, although Black's position is solid enough. One recent practical example continued 16...♕d7 17 d4 exd4 18 cxd4 cxd4 19 ♘xd4 ♖ac8 20 ♗e3 ♘e5 21 ♕b3 ♘c4 with a roughly level position, Kovacevic-Grischuk, Dos Hermanas (blitz) 2003.

15...♗xf5!

Now Black also exchanges for structural advantages: obtaining a pawn preponderance in the centre and saddling White with a vulnerable pawn on f5, which can only be protected at a cost of further weakening with g2-g4. Of course I have to admit that this is almost certainly an over-simplification of a complex position in which White also has trumps (the bishop pair), but overall I think that Black can feel happy.

16 exf5 ♕d7 17 g4 h6

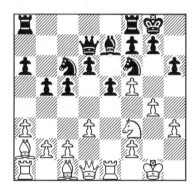

Preventing any ideas of g4-g5 and securing an edge. Adams's play in the remainder of the game is very pleasing.

18 c3 ♖fe8 19 b4 cxb4 20 cxb4 ♗d8 21 ♗b2 a5 22 bxa5 ♗xa5 23 ♖e2 ♗b6 24 ♕b3 ♕b7 25 ♕d1 ♖a4 26 ♖c2 ♘e7 27 ♘h2 ♘ed5 28 ♕f3 ♖f4 29 ♕g2 e4 30 ♖e1 ♖xf2 31 ♖xf2 ♘f4 32 ♕g3 ♗xf2+ 33 ♔xf2 ♘xd3+ 34 ♔f1 ♘xb2 35 h4 ♕d7 36 ♔g2 ♘d3 37 ♖f1 e3 38 g5 hxg5 39 hxg5 ♘h5 0-1

Matching, similar and unlike exchanges

In this chapter I generally deal with exchanges that are matching (bishop for bishop, rook for rook etc.) and ones that are similar (bishop for knight etc.). However, mention should also be made of examples that could be called 'unlike exchanges' but are more likely to be categorised as positional sacrifices; for example, rook for bishop or knight, queen for rook and bishop etc.

Perhaps it's again worth quoting Botvinnik at the point: 'Beautiful games can only take place between masters, since they exchange not only the average, invariable value of the piece, but also its real value, corresponding to the real strength of the piece at a given moment in the game. The average value is obvious; the real value is hidden. Only a deep analysis can reveal the real value of a piece. This depth of analysis gives an aesthetically satisfying sensation to the chessplaying public.'

Appreciation of the 'real' value of pieces is one of the strengths that separate the best players in the world from the rest of the crowd. Garry Kasparov has this ability in abundance, and this is amply shown in the following example, where the world number one dumbfounds both his opponent and the chessplaying public with a very deep 'exchange'.

Kasparov-Shirov
Horgen 1994
Sicilian Defence

1 e4 c5 2 ♘f3 e6 3 d4 cxd4 4 ♘xd4 ♘f6 5 ♘c3 ♘c6 6 ♘db5 d6 7 ♗f4 e5 8 ♗g5 a6 9 ♘a3 b5 10 ♘d5 ♗e7 11 ♗xf6 ♗xf6 12 c3 ♗b7 13 ♘c2 ♘b8 14 a4 bxa4 15 ♖xa4 ♘d7 16 ♖b4 ♘c5

An interesting rook manoeuvre by Kasparov, but it's only after his next move that we see what he is really up to.

17 ♖xb7!!

I've awarded one exclamation mark for the strength of the move and one for the shock value, and even here I could be accused of being a trifle stingy! It's difficult to imagine anyone else in the chess world coming up with such an amazing concept. However, if you can just for a moment force yourself to ignore the traditional value of pieces and look at the real value of the rook and bishop in this situation then Kasparov's move begins to make considerable sense.

Let's look at what the exchange of pieces achieves from White's point of view. Firstly, and perhaps most importantly, Kasparov has put an end to Black's one major idea: fighting for control of the light squares, in particular e4 and d5. Black's whole game-plan since playing 12...♗b7 has been to attack these important squares and with 17 ♖xb7 and White's next move (18 b4!) Kasparov obliterates this idea and leaves Black with absolutely no play. Secondly, Black is left with what you could term as (if you can pardon my English) two (!) worst placed pieces: the knight on b7 and the bishop on f6. The rest of the game witnesses Shirov in the impossible job of trying to improve these miserable beings; even a player of his class has little chance of doing so.

So White has gained an awful amount. And all of this for a mere rook – it's not as though White doesn't have another one!

17...♞xb7 18 b4!

The crucial follow-up – Black must not be allowed to get his knight back into the action via c5. Now the knight is stranded on b7, which is a truly appalling square to be on.

18...♝g5 19 ♞a3! 0-0 20 ♞c4 a5 21 ♝d3 axb4 22 cxb4 ♛b8 23 h4!

Accurate play from Kasparov, as Shirov was threatening to gradually re-introduce his knight into the game via d8. Now Black must make a difficult choice: he must either retreat the bishop to the inferior h6-square or block the knight's path with ...♝d8.

23...♝h6 24 ♞cb6 ♜a2 25 0-0 ♜d2

26 ♛f3 ♛a7 27 ♞d7?

27 ♝b5! was stronger, as now Black can stay in the game with 26...♜a8!.

27...♞d8?

Not the most resilient defence. Now White finally recuperates his material losses (that is, if you believe White was ever down materially) and keeps a complete stranglehold on the position.

28 ♞xf8 ♚xf8 29 b5! ♛a3 30 ♛f5! ♚e8 31 ♝c4 ♜c2 32 ♛xh7! ♜xc4 33 ♛g8+ ♚d7 34 ♞b6+ ♚e7 35 ♞xc4 ♛c5 36 ♜a1! ♛d4

36...♛xc4 loses to 37 ♜a7+ ♚e6 38 ♛e8+.

37 ♜a3 ♝c1 38 ♞e3! 1-0

A fantastic display of positional mastery by Kasparov.

Retaining a piece for attacking purposes

When one of your own pieces is opposed by a matching opponent's piece, there are three options: to actively exchange, to do nothing (thus leaving your opponent with the option of exchanging if he or she so wishes), or to actively avoid the exchange by moving away the piece in question. A player will only usually choose the third option if the 'real' value of his piece is greater than that of the opponent's, as this choice obviously entails a loss of a tempo. One major reason for retaining a piece is for 'attacking' purposes.

The following example, which I first saw on Peter Wells's 'Strategy' column in *ChessBase Magazine*, is particularly striking because it contains a rare case of a bishop giving up a long and seemingly important diagonal to an opposing bishop.

Krasenkow-Romanishin
Lvov 2000

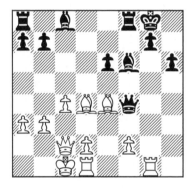

Black has just played the move ...♗e7-f6, preventing the threat on g7 and challenging White's dominance on the a1-h8 diagonal. Krasenkow's reply is outwardly rather surprising but is in fact a profound piece of thinking.

22 ♗e3!

First of all, I'm convinced that there's absolutely nothing wrong with Black's f6-bishop – in fact it looks like a very good defensive piece. However, Krasenkow realises that in this particular position his dark-squared bishop is a major player in his own attack, and here this overrides any other concerns.

22...♕d6?

Krasenkow gives 22...♕c7! 23 ♗xh6 ♕c5 24 d4 ♕xa3+ 25 ♔b1 as Black's only way to stay in the game, although even here I feel that White's attack is very promising.

23 c5 ♕a6 24 a4 ♕a5

Or 24...♔h8 25 ♖g6, preparing ♖h1 and ♗xh6.

25 ♗xh6 ♕b4

Threatening the lethal ...♕a3+, but White gets in the first blow.

26 ♖xg7+!

This leads to a forced win.

26...♗xg7 27 ♗h7+ ♔h8 28 ♗xg7+ ♔xg7 29 ♕g6+ ♔h8 30 ♕h5!

But not 30 ♕h6?? which is met by 30...♕f4! – Krasenkow.

30...♖xf2 31 ♗e4+ ♔g7 32 ♖g1+ ♔f8 33 ♕h6+ ♔e7 34 ♖g7+ ♖f7 35 ♕g5+ ♔e8 36 ♖g8+ 1-0

It's mate after 36...♖f8 37 ♕h5+ ♔e7 38 ♖g7+ ♔d8 39 ♕h4+.

This second example is a bit more extreme. American GM Sergey Kudrin thinks so highly of the attacking powers of his dark-squared bishop that he is willing to give up material to ensure it stays on the board.

Lobron-Kudrin
New York 1983
Sicilian Defence

1 e4 c5 2 ♘f3 d6 3 d4 cxd4 4 ♘xd4
♘f6 5 ♘c3 g6 6 ♗e3 ♗g7 7 f3 0-0
8 ♕d2 ♘c6 9 0-0-0 d5 10 ♘xc6
bxc6 11 ♗h6 e6 12 h4

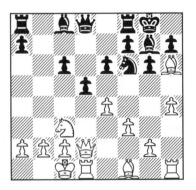

White has offered a typical exchange of bishops with ♗e3-h6. On this particular occasion, however, Kudrin does not play ball.

12...♗h8!

This 'Dragon bishop' is an absolute monster, both in attack, where admittedly Black is certainly helped by the presence of a half-open b-file, but also in defence – every Dragon specialist knows that it's virtually impossible for White to deliver mate down the h-file in the traditional way with this piece still on the board.

13 h5?!

There's a stronger case for either grabbing the exchange immediately with 13 ♗xf8 ♕xf8, followed by grimly trying to hang on for dear life on the queenside, or completely ignoring the rook and carrying on the attack with 13 g4, intending h5. Instead White tries a concoction of both strategies but is ultimately unsuccessful.

**13...♘xh5 14 ♗xf8 ♕xf8 15 g4 ♘g3
16 ♖h3 ♖b8!**

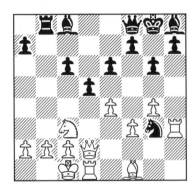

17 a3

17 ♖xg3 fails to 17...♕b4 18 ♕d3 ♗e5 (Byrne/Mednis); for example, 19 ♖g1 ♗f4+ 20 ♖d2 ♗a6! 21 ♕xa6 ♕xb2+ 22 ♔d1 ♕xc3 23 ♕d3 ♗xd2 24 ♕xd2 ♕xf3+ 25 ♔c1 ♕a3+ 26 ♔d1 dxe4, when Black has four pawns and a continuing attack for the bishop.

**17...♗e5! 18 ♕f2 ♗f4+ 19 ♔b1
♘xf1 20 ♖xf1 ♕xa3 21 ♘d1 ♗e5 22
c3 ♗a6! 23 f4 ♗xf1 24 ♕xf1 ♗g7
25 e5 ♕a4 26 ♕f3 g5! 27 fxg5
♗xe5 28 ♕d3 ♕xg4 29 ♕xh7+ ♔f8
30 ♘e3 ♕e2 31 ♘c2 ♔e7 32 ♖e3
♕d1+ 33 ♔a2 ♖h8 0-1**

Before receiving too many complaints from would-be Dragon experts, I would just like to add the disclaimer that this ...♗h8 exchange sacrifice does not always work so successfully!

Retaining a piece for defensive purposes

Actively avoiding an exchange for defensive reasons is a less common idea mainly because, unlike in the game Lo-bron-Kudrin above, a defender may be reluctant to spend a tempo moving a defensive piece from what might already be regarded as its most effective position.

In the following example, however, Black correctly judges that it's worth moving a knight to a seemingly inferior square just to avoid an exchange that would have certainly speeded up White's attack.

Emms-D.Howell

Staunton Memorial, London 2003

Ruy Lopez

1 e4 e5 2 ♘f3 ♘c6 3 ♗b5 a6 4 ♗a4 ♘f6 5 0-0 ♗e7 6 ♖e1 b5 7 ♗b3 0-0 8 a4 ♗b7 9 d3 ♖e8 10 ♘bd2 ♗f8 11 ♘f1 h6 12 ♘e3 ♘a5 13 ♗a2 c5 14 ♗d2 ♘c6 15 c3 ♕c7 16 ♘h4 ♘d8 17 ♘g4

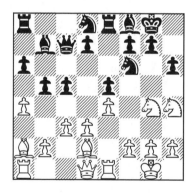

Faced with a daunting defensive task, my young opponent displayed some admirably mature qualities here.

17...♘h7!

There's certainly a temptation to swap off White's aggressive knight with 17...♘xg4? 18 ♕xg4, but on this occa-

sion this merely accelerates White's assault on the black king. After 18...♔h7 White has a number of enticing options, but the direct 19 ♗xh6!! is the easiest way to victory: 19...gxh6 (19...♔xh6 20 ♗xf7 and White mates) 20 ♖e3! ♗e7 (or 20...♗g7 21 ♖g3 ♖g8 22 ♗xf7 ♘xf7 23 ♕f5+ ♔h8 24 ♘g6+ ♔h7 25 ♘f8+ ♔h8 26 ♕h7 mate) 21 ♖g3 ♗g5 22 ♕f5+ ♔h8 23 ♖xg5! hxg5 24 ♕f6+ ♔g8 25 ♘f5 and mate cannot be prevented. It's hardly surprising that lines like the ones above lead to checkmate – there are simply more attacking units than defensive ones.

Following the cool 17...♘h7, however, things are not so clear. The knight on g4 looks impressive, but in many lines it gets in the way of the white queen's path to the kingside. I find some similarities here with the concept of the 'superfluous piece'. For attacking purposes White would like to have both his knight and queen on the g4-square, but of course only one of them is allowed to be on that square at any given moment (see page 53 for more details on this).

18 ♖e3 looks the most logical continuation (it's certainly the most ambitious) but Black's position is surprisingly resilient; for example, 18...c4! (the bishop on c4 must be shut out of the attack) 19 ♖g3 ♔h8 20 ♘f5 ♘e6 and although White has some tempting options, I can't find anything earth-shattering.

Not being able to see anything clear-cut through a direct attack, I opted for a more modest advantage with

18 ♕f3 c4 19 dxc4 bxc4 20 ♖ad1 d6 21 ♕e2 ♖c8 22 ♘e3!? ♗xe4 23 ♗xc4 a5 24 ♗d5

Here White keeps a small plus, but

Black is still very much alive and kicking and in the end I was only able to draw.

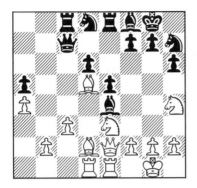

Offering an exchange to open lines

This is a very common idea, especially in the opening and early middlegame. An early pawn capture may have the desired effect of suddenly waking up a dormant rook, as happens with decisive effect in the example below.

Ekstroem-Gaprindashvili

World Team Ch'ship, Lucerne 1997

Sicilian Defence

1 e4 c5 2 c3 d5 3 exd5 ♕xd5 4 d4 ♘f6 5 ♘f3 g6 6 ♕b3!

At first sight it looks a little cowardly for White to offer the exchange of queens so soon, but in fact this is a deceptively difficult move for Black to face. For starters, Black must be wary of ideas including ♗c4 and ♕xd5 followed by grabbing a pawn with dxc5.

6...♕xb3?

I'm convinced that Black has better than this – it simply looks too accommodating. White has succeeded in his ambition of creating a dangerous half-open file for the rook on a1, and this proves to be decisive in the action to come. White has also succeeded in 'speeding his development' with this trade.

The line 6...♗e6 7 c4 ♕d7 8 d5 ♗f5 9 ♘c3 (Emms-Ansell, British League 1999) also looks somewhat better for White, so in my view Black should head for the complications that arise after 6...cxd4! 7 ♗c4! ♕e4+ 8 ♔f1 e6.

7 axb3 cxd4

Or 7...♘bd7 8 dxc5! ♘xc5 9 ♗e3 b6 10 ♗xc5! bxc5 11 ♗b5+ ♗d7 12 ♗xd7+ ♔xd7 13 ♘bd2 and White is better. Black's pawns on the queenside, the one on a7 in particular, are permanent weaknesses and extremely vulnerable.

8 ♘xd4 ♘d5?!

The prophylactic 8...a6! limits the damage, although there is no argument that White has the advantage after 9 ♘b5 ♔d8 10 ♗e3 ♘bd7 11 ♗e2 ♗g7 12 0-0 (Har Zvi).

9 ♗c4 ♘c7 10 ♗f4

Black is already in major trouble, and much of this is down to the half-open a-file. If White's pawn were on a2 instead of b3 then Black's problems would almost disappear.

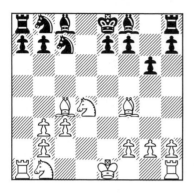

10...♘ba6 11 ♘b5! ♘xb5 12 ♗xb5+ ♔d8?

Black should settle for a pawn deficit after 12...♗d7 13 ♗xa6 bxa6 14 ♖xa6.

13 ♖xa6!

This winning idea is a complete justification of Ekstroem's previous play beginning with 6 ♕b3!.

13...bxa6 14 ♗c6 ♗f5 15 ♔e2 ♗h6

Or 15...♖c8 16 ♖d1+.

16 ♗xh6 ♖b8 17 ♘d2 ♖b6 18 ♗d5 ♗e6 19 ♗xe6 ♖xe6+ 20 ♗e3 ♔c8 21 ♖a1 ♖d8 22 h4 f6 23 b4 ♖d7 24 ♘b3 ♖c6 25 ♘c5 ♖dd6 26 g3 e5 27 h5 g5 28 g4 ♔b8 29 ♔f3 1-0

Exchanging to inflict weaknesses

Exchanging to inflict structural weaknesses on an opponent is, of course, a very common idea. Just think of two quite popular openings: the Exchange Variation of the Ruy Lopez (1 e4 e5 2 ♘f3 ♘c6 3 ♗b5 a6 ♗xc6 dxc6) and the Sämisch Variation of the Nimzo-Indian (1 d4 ♘f6 2 c4 e6 3 ♘c3 ♗b6 4 a3 ♗xc3+ 5 bxc3), where one side trades his bishop for a knight in order to compromise the opponent's pawn structure.

Unless an opponent is simply playing bad moves, you are normally forced to give something in return in this trade. In the case of the Exchange Lopez White gives Black the bishop pair and a ready-made open diagonal for the c8-bishop. In return, as well as creating the pawn weakness, White moves ahead in development (Black has spent a tempo offering the exchange with ...a7-a6). What interests me most are the examples of exchanges in which both sides make obvious concessions. One side accepts serious weaknesses and the other trades a valuable piece or sacrifices material in an unlike exchange. Here judgement obviously plays a vital role and this ability is usually best enhanced by long, hard experience.

In this first example Black accepts the offer to damage White's structure in exchange for 'giving up' a bishop for a knight.

Nevostrujev-Yakovich
Russian Team Ch'ship, Kazan 1995
Sicilian Defence

1 e4 c5 2 ♘f3 d6 3 d4 cxd4 4 ♘xd4 ♘f6 5 ♘c3 g6 6 ♗e2 ♗g7 7 0-0 0-0 8 ♖e1 ♘c6 9 ♘b3 ♗e6 10 ♗f1 a5 11 a4 ♗xb3!? 12 cxb3

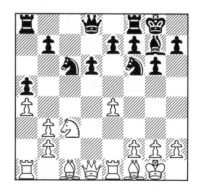

White's structure on the queenside is certainly compromised, but in return Black has traded a bishop for a knight, presenting his opponent with the bishop pair in a reasonably open position and control over some light squares. On this occasion Yakovich justifies Black's decision by following up with dynamic play in the centre.

12...e6!

I'm impressed by the way Yakovich tries to use his extra central pawn and push for ...d6-d5. Black should be able to achieve this advance, especially as it can be supported by the c6-knight jumping to the recently created outpost on b4.

When I first looked at this position, I must admit I was tempted not to touch the central pawns at all, but instead just to place the pieces on good-looking squares. However, in the game Ermenkov-West, Novi Sad Olympiad 1990 this approach was not forcing enough and allowed White to obtain an ideal set-up: 12...♘d7?! 13 ♗e3 ♘c5 14 f3 ♖c8 15 ♗f2 ♘b4 16 ♗c4! e6 17 ♖e2! ♕e7 18 ♖d2 ♖fd8 19 ♕e2 ♗h6 20 ♖dd1 and despite seemingly actively placed pieces, Black cannot improve his position. Crucially, White has a light-squared bind and has a straightforward plan of g2-g3, f3-f4 followed by ♖d2 and ♖ad1, adding further pressure on Black's position.

13 ♗c4 ♘b4 14 ♗g5

Logical play from both sides: Black tries to get in ...d6-d5, and White tries to prevent it.

14...h6 15 ♗xf6?!

I don't really like this move: White gives up the one advantage he had in the pair of bishops. It's true that ...d6-d5 is temporarily prevented, but I don't think

that's a good enough reason for White to give up so much dark-squared control.

I suspect that 15 ♗h4 is stronger, although there's certainly nothing wrong with Black's position after the consistent 15...g5 16 ♗g3 d5! 17 exd5 ♘fxd5.

15...♕xf6 16 ♕d2

Of course 16 ♕xd6? drops the exchange to 16...♘c2.

16...♖fd8 17 ♖ad1 ♔h7 18 ♖e2 d5! 19 exd5 exd5 20 ♗b5

Tactics favour Black in the case of White grabbing on d5; for example, 20 ♘xd5? ♖xd5 21 ♗xd5 ♖d8, or 20 ♗xd5? ♕f5!.

20...♖ac8

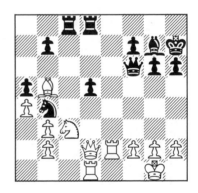

Black has a clear edge: the doubled b-pawns mean that the passed pawn on d5 is virtually a whole extra pawn. The rest of the game sees Yakovich skilfully converting this advantage.

21 ♖ee1 ♖c7 22 ♗d3 ♖e7 23 ♖xe7 ♕xe7 24 ♗b1 ♖e8 25 g3 ♕e5 26 ♘a2 ♘c6 27 ♔g2 d4 28 ♘c1 ♕d5+ 29 f3 ♖e7 30 ♗d3 ♘e5 31 ♗e4 ♕e6 32 ♕xa5 ♘g4 33 ♖d2 ♘e3+ 34 ♔g1 ♕h3 35 ♖f2 d3 36 ♘xd3 ♗d4 37 ♕d8 ♖d7 38 ♕e8 ♘d1 39 g4 ♗xf2+ 40 ♘xf2 ♕h4 41 ♘d3 ♖e7 42 ♕d8 f5 43 gxf5 ♖xe4 0-1

I came across the next example while working on my book *Sicilian Kan*. The exchange that Kobalija employs here is far riskier because Black gives up a traditionally very important defensive bishop that controls the weakened dark squares on the kingside. What is interesting is that although the particular variation with ...g7-g6 and ....&g7 has been around for about 15 years, this was the first example at a high level that I could find where Black opted for this bold trade.

Adams-Kobalija
FIDE World Ch'ship, Las Vegas 1999
Sicilian Defence

1 e4 c5 2 ♘f3 e6 3 d4 cxd4 4 ♘xd4 a6 5 ♗d3 ♘f6 6 0-0 ♕c7 7 ♕e2 d6 8 c4 g6 9 ♘c3 ♗g7 10 ♘f3 0-0 11 ♗f4 ♘bd7 12 ♖fd1 ♘h5 13 ♗e3

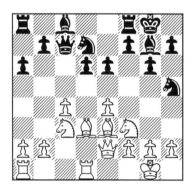

13...♗xc3!?
A visually shocking move, but in all likelihood a good one! Black gives up what is clearly his best minor piece to inflict White with a pair of doubled isolated c-pawns. There are now horrible dark-squared holes near Black's king, but the way Kobalija deals with this problem is quite impressive.

14 bxc3 e5
Immediately Kobalija attempts to regain some control of the dark squares. The bishop may have gone but pawns are ready to take its place.

15 ♗h6 ♖e8 16 ♕e3 ♘c5 17 h3

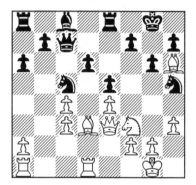

Now in his notes to this game in *Chess Informant*, Adams suggests 17...♗d7, preparing ....♗c6 to attack e4, when I believe that Black is no worse in a very complex position (instead Kobalija played the slightly inferior 17...♗e6). The c-pawns remain weak and for the moment Black has the dark-squared situation on the kingside under control. One option for Black is to bolster the kingside even further with ...f7-f6 and perhaps ...♘g7-e6.

Always lurking in the back of the mind, however, is the fact that at some stage the position could open up, and then Black's long-term weaknesses on the dark squares may be felt – this is in fact the biggest danger for Black. Nevertheless, it's quite revealing that Adams later gave a preference for the move 12 ♖ac1, preventing Black from carrying out this ...♗xc3 idea.

What I like about the following example is the fact that superficially White seems to be getting a good deal from the trade, but a deeper look at the position reveals that he has been hoodwinked!.

Conquest-Tukmakov
Iraklion 1992
Sicilian Defence

1 e4 c5 2 ♘f3 d6 3 d4 cxd4 4 ♘xd4 ♘f6 5 ♘c3 ♘c6 6 ♗c4 e6 7 ♗e3 a6 8 ♕e2 ♕c7 9 f4 ♗e7 10 0-0 0-0 11 a4 ♘xd4 12 ♗xd4 e5 13 ♗e3 ♗e6!

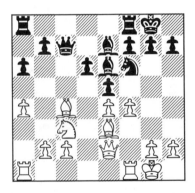

Perhaps those not that familiar with Sicilian Najdorf structures may find this move a little shocking at first. Black offers a trade of bishops and presents White the chance to lumber him with a pair of doubled isolated pawns. Yet this is exactly what Black wants!

14 ♗xe6

Somewhat ironically, I suspect that White should seriously consider the move 14 ♗b3!? here. Then it's Black who has the chance to give White doubled pawns with ...♗xb3, but crucially White keeps some control of the d5 outpost. In *Simple Chess* I looked at many similar Sicilian structures and more often than not the d5-square held the key to the position.

14...fxe6 15 fxe5?

I can see the initial temptation to release the tension and give Black the doubled pawns, but I still don't like it. 15 f5? is answered very strongly by 15...d5!, so I think that White should probably make do with Tukmakov's suggestion of 15 a5!?.

15...dxe5

Doubled isolated pawns rule! Well, they do on this occasion. The change in the structure has benefited Black in two obvious ways:

1) The bishop on e7 has suddenly come alive.

2) The pawns on e6 and e5 cover some crucial squares, including the very important one on d5.

A significant consequence of this second point is that now White is lumbered with the most ineffective minor piece on the board: that knight on c3. It no longer has the option of leaping into d5 and is left without any future apart from the chore of defending the vulnerable e4-pawn.

As for the actual weakness of the pawns, they are not so vulnerable simply because they are not that easy to attack (for one thing, White's e4-pawn gets in the way a bit).

The way Tukmakov takes control of the game from here is quite enlightening. **16 a5 Iac8 17 Ia4 &c5 18 h3 ᐁh5 19 Ixf8+ Ixf8 20 &xc5 Wxc5+ 21 &h2 ᐁf4 22 Wd2 h5**

Looking at the relative activity of the pieces that remain, there's no disputing who has advantage. Tukmakov continues purposefully and is rewarded.
23 ᐁd1 Wc7 24 ᐁe3 Id8 25 Wf2 Id4 26 Ia1 Ixe4 27 Wf3 Id4 28 If1 Id2 29 &h1 Wc6 30 Wxc6 bxc6 31 b4 ᐁd5 32 ᐁc4 Ixc2 33 ᐁxe5 ᐁxb4 34 ᐁd7 Id2 35 If8+ &h7 36 ᐁc5 Id5 37 ᐁxe6 Ixa5 38 h4 Ie5 39 Ie8 &g6 40 ᐁf4+ &f5 41 ᐁxh5 Ixe8 42 ᐁxg7+ &g4 43 ᐁxe8 a5 44 ᐁd6 a4 45 ᐁc4 ᐁc2 46 g3 a3 47 ᐁxa3 ᐁxa3 48 &g2 ᐁc4 49 &f2 c5 50 &e2 ᐁe5 51 &e3 &f5 52 h5 ᐁg4+ 53 &d3 &e5 0-1

The final two examples in this section deal with a common positional sacrifice: trading a rook for a bishop (or knight) in order to inflict doubled isolated pawns on the e-file.

Adorjan-Vadasz
Hungary 1970
Caro-Kann Defence

1 e4 c6 2 d4 g6 3 ᐁf3 &g7 4 c3! d5 5 ᐁbd2 ᐁd7 6 &d3 dxe4 7 ᐁxe4 ᐁgf6 8 ᐁxf6+ ᐁxf6 9 0-0 0-0 10 Ie1 Ie8 11 &g5 Wb6 12 Wd2 &e6?

I believe that Black should avoid giving White the possibility of playing Ixe6. Instead of the text move, 12...&g4! comes to mind. Then after 13 ᐁe5 Black can safely retreat with 13...&e6. This is another example of inducement (see Chapter 1).

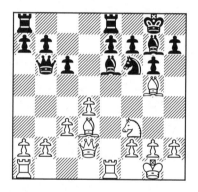

13 Ixe6!
Adorjan cannot resist the temptation, and I'm convinced his judgement is spot on.
13...fxe6
How much compensation does White have in return for giving up rook for bishop? Perhaps it's easiest to list the advantages that White has gained here:

1) Black is saddled with a pair of doubled isolated pawns that, in contrast to the Conquest-Tukmakov example above, are vulnerable to attack, especially down the half-open e-file and on the a2-g8

diagonal.

2) Black has lost a valuable light-squared defender.

3) White can use the outpost on e5.

4) White has a very straightforward plan of a direct attack against Black's weakened kingside.

All in all, this looks like a very good deal for White.

14 ♖e1 c5

Black finds it very difficult to defend e6.

15 ♗c4! ♘d5 16 ♗h6! ♖ad8?

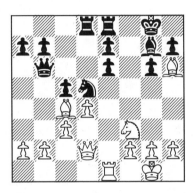

After this move Black's position crumbles. There are more resilient defences, including this pretty variation given by Adorjan in his notes to *Chess Informant*: 16...♖f8! 17 ♗xg7 ♔xg7 18 ♘g5 ♘c7 19 ♖xe6!! ♘xe6 20 ♘xe6+ ♔h8 21 dxc5! (Black is two exchanges ahead but he is totally lost) 21...♕c6 22 ♕d4+ ♖f6 23 g4! g5 24 h4 h6 25 hxg5 hxg5 26 ♕e5! and Black has no good defence to the threat of ♕h2+ followed by a decisive discovered check on the a2-g8 diagonal.

17 ♗xg7 ♔xg7 18 ♘g5 ♘c7 19 ♕f4!

Setting up an enormous family fork.

19...♖f8 20 ♕xc7! ♕xc7 21 ♘xe6+ ♔h6 22 ♘xc7 ♖c8 23 ♘e6 ♖f6 24 g4 1-0

Filippov-Luther

European Championship, Istanbul 2003

Slav Defence

1 ♘f3 ♘f6 2 c4 c6 3 d4 d5 4 ♘c3 a6 5 c5 ♘bd7 6 ♗f4 ♘h5 7 e3 g6 8 ♗d3 ♗g7 9 0-0 0-0 10 ♗g5 ♖e8 11 e4 dxe4 12 ♗xe4 ♘df6 13 ♗c2 ♗e6 14 ♖e1 ♘d5 15 ♕d2 ♕c7 16 ♖xe6!? fxe6

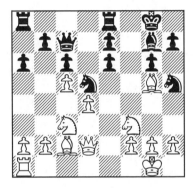

In this example Black is better placed defensively to deal with the direct attack, but I'm convinced that Filippov's decision to go ahead with the exchange sacrifice was still correct, for psychological reasons if nothing else. White is rewarded with a slow-burning initiative, and Black's position is very difficult to handle.

17 ♖e1 ♕d7 18 ♘e5! ♗xe5 19 ♖xe5 ♘g7 20 h4

The e6-square is protected well enough, so White begins an attack on a second front.

20...♖ad8 21 ♘xd5 exd5 22 ♕e2 ♖c8 23 g4! ♖f8 24 h5 gxh5

Here Filippov played 25 gxh5? and eventually won the game, although the position is not totally clear at this point. Instead I prefer the direct 25 ♕d3!. Now I can't see anything better for Black than 25...♕xg4+ 26 ♔f1 ♘f5 27 ♖xf5 ♖xf5 28 ♕xf5 ♕xf5 29 ♗xf5, but this ending must be winning for White – the two bishops are simply too powerful for the rook.

Offering a trade to gain structural advantages

This idea is slightly different to the one discussed in the previous section in that, if the exchange is accepted (it's not always forced), it involves an improvement of a player's structure rather than the deterioration of his opponent's. Let's begin with a relatively simple case.

Smirin-Vaganian
USSR 1988
French Defence

1 e4 e6 2 d4 d5 3 ♘c3 ♗b4 4 ♕d3 ♘e7 5 ♗g5 0-0 6 ♘f3 ♗xc3+ 7 bxc3 f6 8 ♗d2 b6 9 ♕e3 ♗b7 10 ♗d3 dxe4 11 ♗xe4 ♘f5 12 ♕e2 ♗xe4 13 ♕xe4

Here both sides have weaknesses: White has doubled c-pawns and Black has a backward pawn on e6. However, Vaganian is able to eliminate his weakness in a straightforward way.

13...♕d5!

Offering to exchange queens on d5, after which Black rids himself of the weakness of the backward e6-pawn. This scenario is difficult for White to avoid. He cannot protect the queen on e4, and if he tries to keep the queens on the board then he loses valuable time, and Black is able to exploit this. For example, 14 ♕d3 ♘c6! (threatening to obtain a firm grip on the c4-square with ...♘a5) 15 c4 ♕d7 16 c3 e5 17 d5? e4! and Black wins material.

14 ♕xd5 exd5 15 ♗f4 ♘c6! 16 0-0-0

White can grab a hot pawn with 16 ♗xc7, but Black gets a strong initiative after 16...♖ac8 17 ♗f4 ♘a5 18 ♗d2 ♖fe8+ 19 ♔d1 ♘d6 (Vaganian), intending ...♘e4 or ...♘b5 to regain the pawn with advantage.

16...♘a5 17 ♖he1

Now Vaganian erred with 17...♔f7?!, and after 18 g4! ♘d6 19 ♗xd6 cxd6 20 ♘h4 Black was only slightly better.

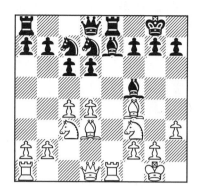

After the game he recommended the improvement 17...h5!, crucially securing the position of the f5-knight. Vaganian's analysis runs 18 ♖e6 ♖fe8 19 ♖de1 ♖xe6 20 ♖xe6 ♔f7 21 ♖e1 ♖c8, when I'm a real fan of Black's position. White's queenside weaknesses will not go away, and Black can play on either side of the board with ...c5 or ...g5 and ...h5.

I remember that Ian Rogers' play in the following game made quite an impression on me at the time. I found it enlightening how he used two exchanges to give him substantially more influence in the centre of the board.

Emms-Rogers

Lloyds Bank Masters, London 1991
Alekhine's Defence

1 e4 ♘f6 2 e5 ♘d5 3 d4 d6 4 ♘f3 ♗g4 5 ♗e2 c6 6 c4 ♘c7 7 exd6 exd6 8 0-0 ♗e7 9 ♘c3 0-0 10 h3 ♗f5 11 ♗f4 ♖e8 12 ♖e1 ♘d7 13 ♗d3

I expected my opponent to capture on d3, after which White's extra space would offer a small advantage. Instead Rogers played...

13...♗g6!

Keeping the tension. Now I saw no reason not to exchange on g6, but perhaps I should have kept the tension myself with something like 14 ♕d2.

14 ♗xg6 hxg6

Naturally capturing towards the centre. Now Black has doubled pawns but they are in no way vulnerable to attack. The significant plus that Black has gained out of the exchange is some control of the f5-square, and this becomes quite important later on.

15 ♕d3 ♘f6 16 ♗h2?!

This move looks a bit wet. Probably I should have expanded with 16 d5.

16...a6 17 ♖ac1 b5!

Black begins a light-squared strategy.

18 a3 ♕d7 19 ♘d2 ♖ad8 20 b4 ♕f5!

This move is possible as a direct consequence of 13...♗g6!.

21 ♕xf5 gxf5

I was beginning to feel uncomfortable here and I suspect that Black is already better – his capturing towards the centre is now beginning to pay dividends. The pawn that was initially on h7 is now playing an important role in the centre of the board. It's much more involved in the game than, say, White's pawn on h3.

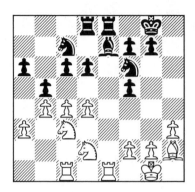

22 ♘b3?! ♘e6 23 ♖ed1 bxc4! 24 ♘a5 d5 25 ♘xc6 ♖d7 26 ♘a4 f4!

The pawn continues to play a starring role: now it blocks out the h2-bishop.

27 ♘xe7+ ♖dxe7 28 ♔f1 g5 29 g3

I had to try to get my bishop back in the game.

29...g4! 30 gxf4 gxh3 31 ♖c3 ♘xd4!

As far as I remember, I think I missed this!

32 ♖g3+

Of course not 32 ♖xd4 ♖e1 mate!

32...♔f8 33 ♖xh3

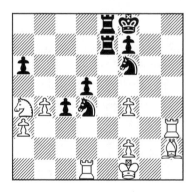

Fortunately for me, Rogers now erred with 33...♘f5? and after 34 ♘b6! I won one of the crucial central pawns and

managed to draw the game. However, after 33...♘c2! the pawns on c4 and d5 promise Black excellent winning chances.

Avoiding an exchange to leave an opposing piece ineffective

There are certainly many instances in which it is desirable to actively avoid the trade of matching or similar pieces. One obvious type of example that comes to mind is when the opponent possesses a very ineffective piece (for example, a conventionally 'bad' bishop that is also bad in the real sense!). The case below is a rather transparent one.

This is admittedly a rather extreme and one-sided example. Black's bishop is traditionally 'bad' and in this position it's certainly worth White keeping the bishops on the board. Indeed, 1 ♗xd7? allows Black to escape with a draw; for example, 1...♔xd7 2 ♔e3 ♔e8 3 ♔f4 ♔f7 4 g4 hxg4 5 ♔xg4 ♔f8 6 ♔g5 ♔g7 7 h5 gxh5 8 ♔xh5 ♔h7 and White cannot make any progress.

1 ♗c2! ♔f7

Or 1...♗e8 2 ♗d3 and White wins the a-pawn.

2 ♗d3 ♗c8 3 ♔c3

and with Black's king tied to the defence of the g6-pawn, the bishop on c8 can only look on helplessly as White's king enters on the dark squares.

Much more interesting is the occasion in which an opponent's piece is outwardly active. In most examples of this an exchange, if on offer, would seem the sensible way forward. However, in some instances the superficially active piece may actually be cut off from the rest of its army and in itself be vulnerable to attack. This can especially happen with knights, as in the following two examples.

Movsesian-Markos
Czech Team Championship, Czechia
2002
Sicilian Defence

1 e4 c5 2 ♘f3 ♘f6 3 ♘c3 d5 4 ♗b5+ ♗d7 5 ♗xd7+ ♕xd7 6 e5 ♘e4

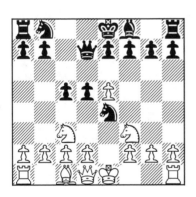

Okay, so it's true that this is an active square for the knight, but on the other hand there are absolutely no retreat squares available from e4 at the moment, and of course White has the possibility

of a later d2-d3.

Black could have avoided the problems he encounters in this game with the counter 6...d4!.

7 ♘e2!

A clever knight retreat to avoid the exchange. Now there is an immediate threat of d2-d3 winning a piece.

7...c4

Black hasn't too many playable options – this one offering the knight a retreat square on c5. Another possibility for Black was to provide a protected retreat square on g5 with 7...h6, the point being that following 8 d3 ♘g5 9 ♘xg5 hxg5 10 ♗xg5, 10...♕g4 wins the pawn back via a double attack on g5 and g2. However, White can continue with 8 h4!?, when once again Black faces the same threat of d2-d3.

8 b4!

I like the way Movsesian continues to encircle the knight. Now the c5-square is covered and the threat of d2-d3 is renewed.

8...cxb3 9 axb3 ♘c6 10 0-0 h6 11 d3 ♘g5

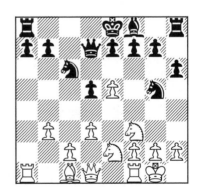

12 ♘fd4!

I find this a nice echo of White's seventh move. Again Movsesian avoids the exchange, preferring to leave the black knight badly placed on g5. Now he will gain more time by attacking the unfortunate piece with f2-f4. The tactical justification behind this move is that 12...♘xe5 drops a piece to 13 f4.

12...g613 ♘xc6 bxc6 14 f4 ♘e6 15 f5!

Using another attack to engineer a pawn break and open the f-file for the rook.

15...gxf5 16 ♖xf5 ♗g7 17 ♘g3 ♘d4 18 ♖h5 ♕e6 19 ♗f4 f6 20 ♕d2 fxe5 21 ♖e1 e4 22 dxe4 dxe4 23 c3! ♘xb3 24 ♕c2 ♕c4 25 ♘f5 0-0 26 ♖xe4 1-0

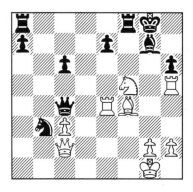

The only way Black can keep the knight is with the amusing 26...♘a1 (completing a neat path of ...♘g8-f6-e4-g5-e6-c5-b3-a1!) but then White wins with 27 ♘xe7+ ♔f7 28 ♕b1 ♕xc3 29 ♖f5+ ♗f6 30 ♕d1, when the threat of ♕h5+ is decisive.

Jansa-Gausel
Andorra la Vella 1993
(see following diagram)

Black has just played the move ...♘h5-f4. Superficially you would think that White would be keen to exchange this

piece but...

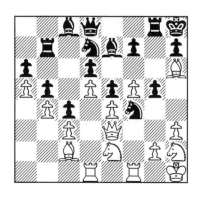

29 ♘g1!

Despite the fact that the knight on f4 has a possible outpost on d3 and a retreat square on h5, it transpires that Black has more problems with it kept on.

29...♗f8 30 ♗xf8 ♕xf8 31 ♖d2 ♘f6?

In his notes in *Chess Informant* Jansa gives this move a question mark, suggesting that Black should retreat without provocation with 31...♘h5.

32 ♗d1! ♕h6 33 ♘g4 ♘xg4 34 ♗xg4

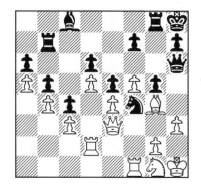

Now White is threatening 35 ♕f3, preventing Black's knight from escaping back via h5. White would then continue with g2-g3, forcing the knight to d3, before winning material with ♕e2-e3 and, finally, ♗g4-e2xd3. Therefore Black is forced to retreat to h5 immediately, but then White can exchange under much better circumstances than before.

34...♘h5 35 ♗xh5!

Eliminating a good defender, which the knight would be back on f6.

35...♕xh5

36 g4

Now Black is left with a horrible bishop on c8 and White has an easy plan of an eventual h3-h4.

36...♕h6 37 ♖h2 f6 38 ♘f3 ♕f8 39 h4, gxh4 40 ♖xh4 ♗bg7 41 ♖g1 ♕f7 42 ♕h6 ♗d7 43 g5 ♗xf5!

The only chance.

44 exf5 fxg5

45 ♖hg4!

But not 45 ♘xg5? ♖xg5!! 46 ♖xg5 ♕xd5+ 47 ♔h2 ♕d2+, when White cannot avoid perpetual check.

45...♕xd5 46 ♖1g3 ♕d1+ 47 ♘g1 ♕d5+ 48 ♔h2 e4 49 ♕f6 ♕f7 50 ♕xf7 ♖xf7 51 ♖xg5 ♖gf8 52 ♖3g4 d5 53 ♖f4 ♖g7 54 ♖xg7 ♔xg7 55 ♘e2 ♔f6 56 ♔g3 h5 57 ♘d4 ♖g8+ 58 ♔f2 ♖h8 59 ♖h4 ♔g5 60 ♔g3 ♖h6 61 ♖h1 h4+ 62 ♔h3 ♔f4 63 ♖g1 ♔e3 64 ♖g6 ♖h8 65 ♖xa6 ♔d3 66 ♘xb5 e3 67 ♖e6 1-0

The superfluous piece

In *Simple Chess* I spent a chapter looking at the different characteristics of an outpost, which I classified as a square where it is possible to establish a piece which cannot easily be attacked by opposing pawns. Here I would briefly like to go back to the subjects of outposts and, more specifically, the 'superfluous piece'.

As I illustrated in *Simple Chess*, when both sides are battling over an outpost, it's very common for there to be a mass of exchanges on the particular square until finally one side is declared the winner. Either the outpost is occupied by the only remaining piece battling for the square or the initial possessor of the outpost loses control over that square or a more important area of the board.

However, if one side sees that he is easily losing the battle for the control of an outpost, there is an alternative approach, which was classified very neatly by Dvoretsky: 'In the fight for a given square players most often try to exchange these pieces off. But sometimes a totally different strategy is adopted: if the square cannot be won by means of exchanges, then one may ... forget about exchanges altogether (after all, only one of the opponent's pieces will be able to occupy the "important high ground", and the others will turn out to be, so to speak, superfluous).'

Although I believe Dvoretsky was the first to actually categorise this idea of the 'superfluous piece' (a term that is becoming more and more trendy in chess writing), the concept had been discussed before. I first came across this notion when reading Jan Timman's comments in a game that he annotated for the book *Learn from the Grandmasters*. I was only just in my teens when I first read it, so I found some of the more refined ideas went over my head, but I do remember that Timman's words left an impression on me.

Timman-Balashov
Sochi 1973

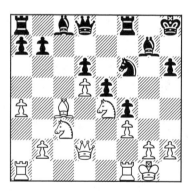

Timman wrote: '...Spassky uttered the opinion that it might have been advisable for White to exchange one of his knights, because after the text move [20 ♗d3] Black can continue with 20...♘e8, leaving White with two knights protecting each other. Although he was not at

all sure about it, his opinion struck me because I had been thinking about that during the game, but then I rejected 20 ♘xf6 not wanting Black's dark-squared bishop to come into play after 20...♗xf6. After all, it is not only Black who is weak on the light squares, also White is just as weak on the dark squares; the only thing is that Black cannot derive any profit from it at the moment. It is not possible to transfer the poor bishop at g7 to the diagonal g1-a7.'

The only problem with this practical example is the fact that, as Timman mentions, it's not really a clear-cut enough case: there are both pros and cons in White exchanging knights. But it does show that the idea of the superfluous piece is not completely new (not that anyone was denying this).

The Rumanian grandmaster Mihai Suba creates a much more unambiguous example of the superfluous piece (one that is quite difficult to improve upon) in his thought-provoking book *Dynamic Chess Strategy.*

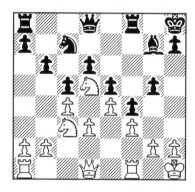

Talking about the above position, Suba states, 'White to move should play 1 ♘xc7 ♕xc7 2 ♘d5 with a clear advantage of a dominant knight against a bad bishop and automatic play on the queen-side with b4, bxc5 etc. Black to move should avoid the exchange and make the knight on c3 superfluous, for example 1...♘e6, keeping the game alive with good counterchances on the kingside.'

If the Timman game was unclear, in this example there really is no question what each side should play if they had the move. Black's decision is simplified even further by the fact that the black knight has a potential outpost itself on d4. By playing 1...♘e6 Black also once again leaves the two white knights protecting each other. I imagine to the beginner this would seem like an ideal state for a pair of knights to be in, but most experts would agree that this is certainly not the case. In the book *Improve Your Chess Now* the Norwegian GM Jonathan Tisdall writes that the knight pair are never happy protecting each other. 'Then they step on each other's hooves, and reduce their own range. When protecting each other they often become paralysed in this configuration. They are best when employed side by side, when they can influence a virtual barrier of squares.'

I particularly like the following example because it shows that it's not just a pair of knights that can get in each other's way.

Rublevsky-Ernst
Helsinki 1992
Sicilian Defence

1 e4 c5 2 ♘c3 ♘c6 3 ♘ge2 e5

Showing a remarkable disdain for the d5-square!

4 ♘d5 d6 5 ♘ec3 ♘ge7 6 ♗c4 ♘xd5 7 ♘xd5 ♗e7 8 d3 0-0 9 0-0

♗e6 10 f4 exf4 11 ♗xf4 ♘e5 12 ♔h1 ♗g5 13 ♗xe5 dxe5 14 ♕f3 ♔h8 15 ♕g3 f6 16 ♗b3 ♖c8 17 ♖ad1 ♕e8 18 ♘c3

Ernst's next move shows a deep appreciation of the position.

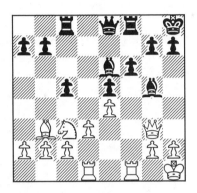

18...♗d7!

It's true that with this move Black keeps both the bishop pair and his traditionally 'good' bishop, but there is actually much more to Ernst's thinking. By refusing to exchange his bishop for White's bishop on b3 (or for the knight on d5 earlier), Black leaves White with a superfluous piece. Both of White's minor pieces would like to occupy the d5-square, but of course there is only room for one of them. If the knight leaps into d5 then the scope of the bishop on b3 is severely reduced, while if the bishop occupies d5 then the knight will have to look elsewhere for a new post. In contrast, 18...♗xb3? 19 axb3 followed by ♘d5 would give White an obvious advantage.

The idea of the superfluous piece can be expanded to include examples without the existence of a traditional outpost. In these cases there is more than a passing similarity to the idea of avoiding exchanges to leave an opponent's piece vulnerable (see page 50).

Ponomariov-Graf
European Team Ch'ship, Plovdiv 2003
Ruy Lopez

1 e4 e5 2 ♘f3 ♘c6 3 ♗b5 a6 4 ♗a4 ♘f6 5 0-0 ♗e7 6 ♖e1 b5 7 ♗b3 d6 8 c3 0-0 9 h3 ♘a5 10 ♗c2 c5 11 d4 ♘d7 12 ♘bd2 exd4 13 cxd4 ♘c6 14 d5 ♘ce5

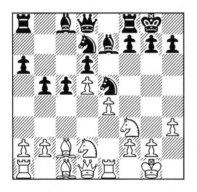

In this example Black would be quite happy to exchange off one of his knights, otherwise they may, as Tisdall would say, begin to 'step on each other's hooves'. Ponomariov decides to leave Black with exactly this problem.
15 ♘h2!?
15 ♘xe5 ♘xe5 16 f4 is the obvious continuation, but it seems that the exchange of one set of minor pieces improves Black's overall position. I must admit that after 16...♘g6 17 ♘f3 f5! 18 e5 dxe5 19 fxe5 ♗b7 20 d6 White's pawns in the centre look very daunting, but in the game Ponomariov-Beliavsky, Moscow (rapid) 2002, the ex-Soviet GM showed that the pawns were also vulner-

able to attack after 20...♗h4 21 ♖e2 ♗g3!.

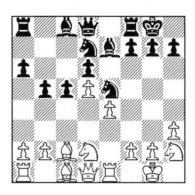

After 15 ♘h2!? Graf became so intent on preventing f2-f4 that he played the rather committal **15...g5?!**, but following **16 ♘df1!** White suddenly has the f5-outpost at his disposal and is clearly on top.

I came across another example of the superfluous piece when studying a reasonably well known line of the Closed Sicilian.

1 e4 c5 2 ♘c3 ♘c6 3 g3 g6 4 ♗g2 ♗g7 5 d3 d6 6 f4 e6 7 ♘f3 ♘ge7 8 0-0 0-0 9 ♗e3 ♘d4 10 e5 ♗d7 11 ♘e4 ♘ef5 12 ♗f2

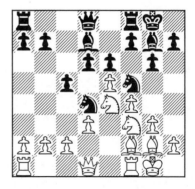

I was analysing this variation with the intention of playing it with black pieces and was unsure whether Black should play the move 12...♗c6?! or 12...♘xf3+! followed by 13...♗c6, regardless of how White recaptured on f3. At first glance I was in favour of an immediate **12...♗c6?!**, as I believed it kept more options available for Black, but then I became uneasy about the fact that Black's position was full of superfluous pieces! The knights on f5 and d4 are, in that negative sense, protecting each other, while by playing 12...♗c6?!, Black deprives the knight on d4 of a retreat square on c6. Eventually I noticed that with the clever move **13 ♘fd2!**, suddenly the knight on d4 becomes vulnerable to attack with c2-c3. Black's play looks quite forced from here: **13...dxe5 14 fxe5 ♗xe5 15 ♘c4 ♗g7 16 c3 ♘b5 17 ♗xc5**

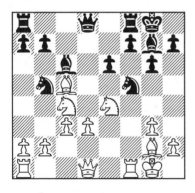

with a better position for White, whose pieces are very active.

When I later looked up the line on my chess database, I noticed that, although 12...♘xf3+ was the most common move, the position after 12...♗c6 had arisen on over thirty occasions, some involving grandmasters. However, in only three

games did White play the critical 13 ♘fd2!. More common were 13 c3 and 13 g4, both of which suit Black perfectly after 13...♘xf3+ and 14...♘d4. Perhaps this has something to do with a player's instinctive reluctance to analyse knight retreats (see Chapter 3 for more on this).

Considering the strength of the remaining pieces

If play is taken into the endgame, decide which pieces it is necessary to retain, and exchange those that are unnecessary. – Capablanca

I guess you could say that it's absolutely irrelevant which pieces you choose to exchange because the only important thing is what's left on the board (pieces that leave the board won't win you the game!). The ability to carry out apparently strange or illogical exchanges in recognition of the importance of what remains separates the special from the merely very good. There has already been a few examples in this chapter (Fischer-Petrosian and Kasparov-Shirov spring to mind), but here are a couple more. In the first White correctly, in my opinion, gives up two of his most active pieces to reach a technically winning endgame, whereas in the second example White wrongly allows an exchange of a queen and a pawn for two rooks.

Korchnoi-Suetin
Budva 1967
Queen's Gambit Accepted

1 d4 d5 2 c4 dxc4 3 e4 ♘f6 4 e5 ♘d5 5 ♗xc4 ♘c6 6 ♘e2 ♘b6 7 ♗d3 ♗e6 8 ♘bc3 ♕d7 9 ♘e4 ♘b4 10

♗b1 ♗c4 11 ♘c5 ♕g4 12 h3 ♕xe2+ 13 ♕xe2 ♗xe2 14 ♔xe2 0-0-0 15 e6 ♘c6 16 ♗e3 f6 17 ♗e4 g6

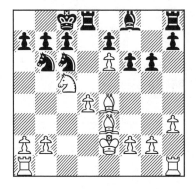

I imagine that White has a few ways to exploit his obvious positional advantage, but the one chosen here by Korchnoi is outwardly rather surprising. Who would have thought that White would want to trade his wonderfully placed bishop on e4 and knight on c5 for a mere rook and pawn?

18 ♘xb7! ♔xb7 19 ♖ac1 ♖d5

The try 19...♘d5 runs into the reply 20 ♖c5!.

20 ♗xd5 ♘xd5 21 ♖c5! ♘xe3 22 fxe3

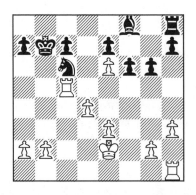

Korchnoi has exchanged two of his best pieces off the board, but of course the only relevant thing is what pieces remain. In fact the position has clarified somewhat and it's easy to see that White is still left with a clear advantage, despite the approximate material equality. White's rooks and pawns run rampant, while Black's pieces, the knight and bishop in particular, struggle to make any kind of impact on the game.

22...♗h6 23 ♖d1 ♖d8 24 ♖d3 ♘b8 25 ♖b3+ ♔c8 26 ♖bc3 c6 27 b4 f5 28 b5

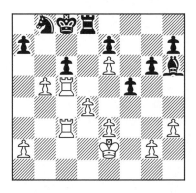

That knight on b8 is not a happy piece! In the end the best that Suetin can do is to sacrifice it for a couple of pawns, and Korchnoi makes the rest of the game look very easy.

28...f4 29 d5 fxe3 30 g3 ♖f8 31 ♖c2 ♖f2+ 32 ♔d3 ♖f1 33 dxc6 ♔c7 34 ♖d5 ♖f2 35 ♖xf2 exf2 36 ♔e2 ♗e3 37 a4 a6 38 ♖d3 ♗c5 39 ♖f3 axb5 40 axb5 h6 41 ♖f8 g5 42 ♖h8 ♗d6 43 ♔xf2 ♔b6 44 ♖d8 ♔c7 45 ♖f8 ♔b6 46 ♖f5 ♘xc6 47 bxc6 ♔xc6 48 ♔f3 ♗b4 49 ♖e5 ♗d6 50 ♖e3 ♔d5 51 ♔g4 ♗e5 52 ♖e2 ♗d6 53 h4 gxh4 54 gxh4 ♗e5 55 ♔f5 ♗f6 56 ♖d2+ ♔c6 57 h5 ♗g5 58 ♖d7 ♔c5 59 ♔g6 1-0

McDonald-Webb
British League, Birmingham 1998
Sicilian Defence

1 e4 c5 2 ♘f3 d6 3 d4 cxd4 4 ♘xd4 ♘f6 5 ♘c3 g6 6 ♗e3 ♗g7 7 f3 0-0 8 ♕d2 ♘c6 9 0-0-0 ♘xd4 10 ♗xd4 ♗e6 11 ♔b1 ♕c7 12 g4 ♖fc8 13 g5 ♘h5 14 ♗xg7 ♘xg7 15 ♘d5 ♕d7 16 h4 ♖c5 17 f4 ♖ac8

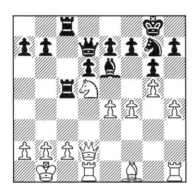

18 ♖h2?
'This looks like a natural move but it just loses,' was grandmaster Neil McDonald's rueful comment after the game. Instead White should prevent Black's idea with the straightforward 18 c3.

18...♗xd5! 19 exd5 ♖xc2! 20 ♕xc2 ♖xc2 21 ♖xc2 ♘h5

Although the material exchange (a queen and a pawn for two rooks) seemed reasonably fair for both sides, in fact what remains on the board is very much in Black's favour. Here his queen and knight complement each other very well and prove to be an irresistible attacking force. White's pawns on the kingside are very difficult to protect (the rooks and bishop are bad defenders here) and are ready for plucking. An-

other problem with White's position is that he has no real counterplay. Neil had been relying on some back rank tricks but it soon becomes apparent that these don't work.

22 ♖d4 ♕g4 23 ♗e2 ♕xh4 24 ♗xh5 gxh5!

White removes the knight in order to safeguard the f4-pawn, but now Black has a very powerful passed pawn to run down the board and this proves to be decisive.

25 a3 ♕g4 26 ♔a2 h4 27 ♖f2 h3 28 ♖dd2 ♕g3 29 ♔b1 ♔g7 30 ♔c2 b5 31 ♖f1 ♕e3 32 ♔d1 ♔g6 33 ♖e2 ♕d3+ 34 ♔e1 ♕g3+ 35 ♔d2 h2 36 f5+

This is desperation from White, but the alternative 36 ♖h1 loses after 36...♕xf4+ 37 ♔d1 ♕d4+ 38 ♔c1 ♕g1+, while 36 ♔c2 ♕g1 37 ♖ee1 ♕c5+ 38 ♔b1 ♕xd5 is also winning for Black.

36...♔xg5 37 f6 exf6 38 ♔c2 ♕g1 39 ♖ee1 ♕g2+ 40 ♔b1 f5 41 ♖c1 f4 0-1

Black will simply move the pawn to f2, place the queen on g1 and then march the king to g2. White can do nothing against this plan.

Exchanging to increase control over a colour complex

Let us suppose that White is trying to increase his control over the light squares in a certain position and he decides that he wants to achieve this through exchanges. One might advise White, if the opportunity arose, to exchange a knight for Black's light-squared bishop. Less obvious, however, is the idea of White exchanging his dark-squared bishop for a black knight. However, this can be just as effective, as the following example demonstrates.

Bach-Schmall
Baden Baden 1993
English Opening

1 g3 c5 2 ♗g2 ♘c6 3 ♘f3 g6 4 c4 ♗g7 5 ♘c3 d6 6 0-0 e5 7 a3 ♘ge7 8 ♖b1 a5 9 d3 0-0 10 ♗g5! h6?

Black should prevent White's idea with 10...f6!, after which White, happy at having induced a slight weakness in Black's camp, retreats with 11 ♗d2 or 11 ♗e3.

11 ♗xe7! ♘xe7

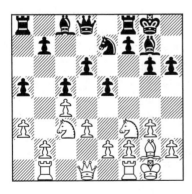

Given that White's central pawns are on light squares, he has just exchanged a traditionally 'good' bishop for a knight. What was the point of this? Well, the strategy White uses in this game very much revolves around controlling some important light squares in the position (for example, e4, d5 etc.). White's dark-squared bishop was his only minor piece that didn't have the potential to control light squares, so it was quite logically traded for one which could (Black's knight on e7). In this way White cleverly uses his dark-squared bishop in the battle for the light squares. In his book *Bishop v Knight*, Steve Mayer called this 'changing the colour of the bishop' and devoted a whole chapter to the idea.

If we look at the remaining minor pieces on the board we see that White has three that can contribute towards the struggle on the light squares while Black really has only two. The bishop on g7 can play no part in this battle, unless it could successfully exchange itself for a white knight – an unlikely possibility.

12 b4

Another attribute of 11 ♗xe7 is that it removed a defender of the b4-square (the knight on c6).

In the game Peelen-So.Polgar, Wijk aan Zee 1990, White chose a more restrained path but the end result was the same. White's domination of the light squares becomes more and more apparent as the game goes on: 12 ♘e1 ♖b8 13 ♘c2 ♗e6 14 b4! cxb4 15 axb4 d5 16 cxd5 ♘xd5 17 ♘xd5 ♗xd5 18 ♗xd5 ♕xd5 19 ♘e3 ♕d8 20 ♕a4! axb4 21 ♖xb4 f5? (it's understandable that Black doesn't merely want to sit passively, but this just weakens the position further) 22 ♖fb1 ♖f7 23 ♕a2! ♔f8 24 ♕e6 ♕f6 25 ♕c4 ♕d8 26 ♖b6 f4 27 ♘d5 g5 28 ♘c3

♜c8 29 ♛b4+ ♔g8 30 ♞e4 30...♝f8 31
♛b3 ♜cc7 32 ♛e6 f3 33 ♛g6+ ♝g7 34
♜d6 ♛f8 35 exf3 ♜xf3 36 ♜e6 ♜e7 37
♜xe7 ♛xe7 38 ♜c1! b5 39 ♜c6! b4 40
♜e6 and Black resigned.

**12...b6 13 ♞e1 ♜a6 14 ♞c2 axb4
15 axb4 ♞f5 16 ♞d5 h5 17 b5 ♝a7
18 ♜a1 ♜xa1 19 ♛xa1 ♝b7 20 ♛a7
♝xd5 21 ♝xd5 ♞e7 22 ♛b7 ♞xd5
23 ♛xd5**

The position has simplified somewhat but this has only served to magnify White's advantage on the light squares. I find it instructive how Black's bishop on g7 remains an admiring spectator while the white knight slowly but surely improves its position.

**23...♝h6 24 ♜a1 ♛c7 25 ♜a6 ♜c8
26 e3 ♔g7 27 ♞a3!**

This knight is coming to d5!

**27...h4 28 ♞b1 hxg3 29 hxg3 ♝g5
30 ♞c3 f5?**

As in the note to White's 12th move, this only quickens the end.

31 ♛e6 1-0

A good time to resign. As soon as White's knight is ready to jump into d5, Black's position collapses. We will look at this idea of colour control more in Chapter 3.

Exchanging to emphasise weaknesses

In *Simple Chess* there were many demonstrations of this theme (in the chapter on isolated queen's pawns, for example), but I would just like to add one further one here. This following game is interesting because it also bring up the aspect of 'space and exchanges'. In *Simple Chess* I acknowledged the common belief that it is often very useful to exchange pieces if you have a space disadvantage, while likewise it is often useful to avoid exchanges if you have a space advantage. In hedgehog positions Black obviously has less space than White, but paradoxically exchanges often favour the player with more space (this has been mentioned before by a few experts). One of the main reasons for this paradox is the glaring weakness of Black's pawns on a6, b6 and d6. In the middlegame they can be protected more easily and even provide Black with dynamic possibilities based on the possible freeing (and normally equalising) advances ...b6-b5 and ...d6-d5. In the endgame, however, they are more likely to simply become liabilities, as we shall now see in the game below.

Adorjan-Phominyh
Balassagyarmat 1990
English Opening

1 c4 ♘f6 2 ♘c3 c5 3 g3 e6 4 ♘f3 b6 5 ♗g2 ♗b7 6 0-0 a6 7 d4 cxd4 8 ♕xd4 d6 9 ♘g5!?

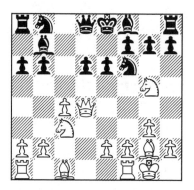

Very simplistic. White offers wholesale exchanges in the hope that Black's obvious pawn weaknesses will be more vulnerable in an ending. In this game this strategy works to perfection.

9...♗xg2 10 ♔xg2 ♕c7?!

Not the best move order. Adorjan himself had previously shown a better way for Black to defend: 10...♗e7 11 ♗e3 ♘bd7 12 ♘ge4 ♕c7 13 ♖fd1 0-0 (Stangl-Adorjan, Altensteig 1989) and now 14 ♘xd6?! ♖ad8! is awkward for White. I wonder what Adorjan had planned if Phominyh had just repeated this.

11 ♘ce4!

More exchanges!

11...♘xe4 12 ♕xe4! ♕c6

Further simplification is virtually forced. If 12...♘c6 then White can cheekily grab a pawn with 13 ♘xh7!.

13 ♖d1 h6 14 ♕xc6+ ♘xc6 15 ♘e4 0-0-0 16 ♗f4 ♔c7 17 ♖ac1

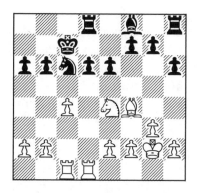

The ending has been reached and White has a clear edge. With all the exchanges, especially the one involving queens, Black's hedgehog position has lost all of its normal dynamic power he is simply left with the boring task of defending his obvious pawn weaknesses.

17...g5 18 ♗e3 ♔b7 19 ♖d3! f5?

Now Black finds himself in real trouble. 19...d5! minimises the damage.

20 ♖b3! fxe4 21 ♗xb6 ♔c8 22 ♗xd8 ♔xd8 23 ♖b6 ♔c7 24 ♖xa6

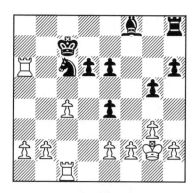

The material situation is still roughly level, but White's queenside pawns are very dangerous.

24...♔b7 25 ♖a4 ♖h7 26 b4 ♖c7 27 c5 ♘a7 28 c6+! ♔b6 29 b5! ♘xb5 30 ♖a8 ♗g7 31 ♖b8+ ♔a6 32 ♖b1

Rxc6 33 R1xb5 &d4 34 Rb4 &a7
35 Re8 e5 36 e3 &c3 37 Ra4+ &b7
38 Re7+ &b6 39 Re6 &c5 40 Rxh6
&d5 41 Rg6 &d2 42 a3 Rb6 43 h4
gxh4 44 gxh4 Rb2 45 &g3 &e1 46
Rf6 Re2 47 &g2 &d2 48 Ra6 1-0

Exercises

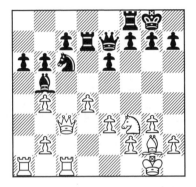

Exercise 2.1 White to play
What is White's most effective move in this position?

Exercise 2.2 Black to play
Can you suggest a good plan for Black?

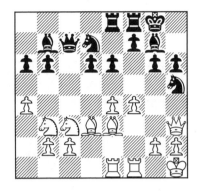

Exercise 2.3 Black to play
Is the provocative 18...&xc3 a good idea here? After 19 bxc3 how should Black continue?

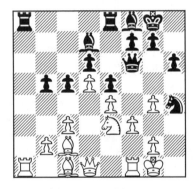

Exercise 2.4 White to play
Black has just offered an exchange of rooks with ...Rb8-a8. White could trade on a8 or keep the tension on the a-file with 26 &d2, intending to recapture on a1 with the queen. Is there a third option?

CHAPTER THREE

Of Minor Importance

In *Simple Chess* I devoted a chapter to the 'bishop pair' and in particular its very common battle against the bishop and knight partnership. Such is the broadness of this particular topic, however, that it was impossible to give it comprehensive coverage. (Whole books, including Steve Mayer's excellent *Bishop v Knight: the verdict*, have been written on the issue of minor pieces.) Thus in this chapter I would like to expand a little on some of the ideas mentioned in my previous book, looking again at how to make the most of the bishop pair and also how to fight against this phenomenon.

The unopposed bishop

One rather evident way of exploiting a bishop pair against a bishop and knight team is to utilise to the full what has been called 'the unopposed bishop', that is the bishop of the same colour complex as the one already exchanged. If, for example, White exchanges his knight for Black's light-squared bishop, then White's own light-squared bishop no longer has a direct opponent and its strength could actually increase due to

this factor. This is exactly what happens in this first example below. It's very much a clear-cut demonstration of the bishop pair possessor taking full advantage of his unopposed bishop, although it has to be said that he does rely on a little help from his opponent!

Benjamin-Balinas
Philadelphia 1994
Pribyl Defence

1 d4 d6 2 ♘f3 ♗g4

From very early on Black signals his intent to exchange this bishop for the knight on f3, most likely in return for structural compensation.

3 c4 ♘d7 4 d5!?

A clever idea. By giving the knight the option of jumping into the d4-square, White puts pressure on Black to make a decision with his bishop.

4...♗xf3

The simplest solution, although 4...e5 is also possible and has been played quite a few times.

5 exf3

Okay, Black has given up the bishop

pair in return for compromising White's pawn structure. The important question is how should he continue from here?

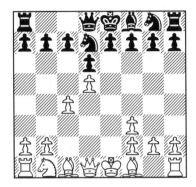

5...e6?

This is certainly not the way forward, and Black should be very wary of moves that allow White to increase the scope of his unopposed bishop without any real effort. It's true that in a few openings, the Classical Nimzo-Indian (1 d4 ♘f6 2 c4 e6 3 ♘c3 ♗b4 4 ♕c2) being a prime example, Black often tries to open the position up after giving up the bishop pair. On many occasions this seemingly paradoxical decision (we know that in general bishops prefer open positions) is justified by another important feature – a lead in development. In this example, however, White has not wasted any time either forcing the exchange or keeping his structure intact. As a consequence there is no lead in development for Black and no other factor to justify his decision.

5...g6! is more sensible, one continuation being 6 ♗d3 ♗g7 7 0-0 ♘gf6 8 ♘c3 0-0 9 ♗g5 (Greenfeld-Finkel, Tel Aviv 2002). I suspect that at some stage Black will probably want to challenge White's pawn with ...c7-c6 or ...e7-e6,

but at least White has already committed his light-squared bishop to a relatively passive square.

6 dxe6! fxe6 7 g3!

Very logical play from Benjamin. The bishop will be very impressively placed on either h3 or (after a timely f3-f4) on g2.

7...♕f6

By opting to castle queenside Black is really playing with fire!

8 ♘c3 0-0-0 9 ♗g2 ♔b8 10 0-0 ♘e7 11 f4 ♘f5

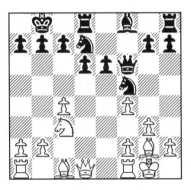

I'm already a big fan of White's position. It's difficult not to notice the influence of White's g2-bishop along the long diagonal.

12 ♘e4 ♕g6 13 a4! ♗e7 14 a5!

Black is beginning to feel a chill on those neglected light squares. White's plan is to play a5-a6, answering ...b7-b6 with ♕a4 and the horrible threat of ♕c6. Black's next move prevents this plan but only at a cost of giving White a 'hook' (the a6-pawn) for his attack on the queenside.

Note that Black could try something similar on the kingside with ...h7-h5-h4, but even after opening the h-file, Black is not going to checkmate White while that

light-squared bishop is still on the board.
14...a6 15 b4!

Consistent, obvious and good.

**15...d5 16 cxd5 exd5 17 ♕xd5 ♘c5
18 ♕a2 ♘d3 19 b5!**

There's no need to prepare this move here. The attack virtually plays itself.

19...axb5 20 a6 ♘b4

After 20...♕xa6 21 ♕xa6 bxa6 22 ♖xa6 (Benjamin) White's attack continues to look ominous even after the queen exchange.

21 ♕b1 bxa6 22 ♗a3 ♖d4 23 ♘c3!

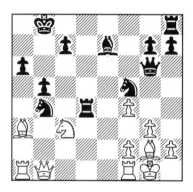

Finally the long diagonal is cleared of all wood and the light-squared bishop's scope is revealed. Black has no chance of dealing with the mounting threats.

**23...c5 24 ♘xb5! axb5 25 ♗xb4
♖xb4 26 ♕d1**

Good enough, but 26 ♕xb4!! cxb4 27 ♖fc1, as given by GM Zapata, would have been a rather nice way to finish the game. I like the way Black's king is sandwiched between the two rooks and bishop.

**26...♖d8 27 ♕f3 ♕b6 28 ♕a8+ ♔c7
29 ♖a7+ ♕xa7**

Or 29...♔d6 30 ♕d5 mate.

30 ♕xa7+ 1-0

It's mate after 30...♔d6 31 ♕b6+ ♔d7

32 ♕c6 – the light-squared bishop plays a crucial role right to the end.

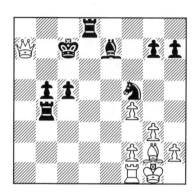

In the following game I opted for a doubled-edged exchange of bishop for knight in order to ruin my opponent's structure. I then made the mistake of allowing the position to open up too quickly and was punished by, amongst other things, the unopposed bishop.

I.Sokolov-Emms
Hastings 1998/99
Queen's Indian Defence

**1 d4 ♘f6 2 c4 e6 3 ♘f3 b6 4 ♘c3
♗b4 5 ♕b3 c5 6 ♗g5 ♗b7 7 ♖d1
0-0 8 e3 cxd4 9 exd4**

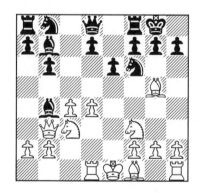

9...♗xf3!?

Given that this is the move I recommended in my book *Easy Guide to the Nimzo-Indian*, I could hardly back down now I had the chance to play it in one of my own games! The temptation to make this exchange is quite strong, as White is saddled with doubled and isolated pawns and his king has apparently no safe place to hide. However, White can hope to exploit the open lines to whip up an attack against Black's king, and there's also the not insignificant matter of White's unchallenged light-squared bishop.

If Black is looking for an easier life then the other bishop-for-knight exchange, 9...♗xc3+ comes into consideration. After 10 ♕xc3 ♘e4 11 ♕e3 ♘xg5 12 ♘xg5 d5 13 ♗d3 h6 14 ♘f3 dxc4 15 ♗xc4 Black is fine. Therefore White should play 10 bxc3, although Black is still okay after the solid 10...d6.

10 gxf3 ♗e7 11 ♖g1 ♖e8 12 ♗e2 d6 13 f4 ♘bd7 14 ♕c2 d5?

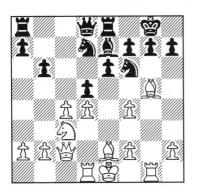

Although during and immediately after the game I felt quite aggrieved that what I considered a natural-looking move landed me with such a miserable position, I now realise that ...d5 is playing right into White's hands, allowing him to open the position and utilise his uncontested bishop. In the post-mortem Sokolov and I decided that the strongest move for Black is 14...♖c8!, planning to answer 15 f5 with 15...e5! to keep the position as blocked as possible. In this way White would find it harder to utilise his extra bishop.

15 f5!

Bold and strong. With the white king there, superficially it seems as though opening the centre carries great risk, but Sokolov correctly assesses that it's White who has all the attacking chances in this position.

15...exf5 16 ♕xf5 dxc4 17 ♗xc4!

Around this point I started to feel rather uncomfortable, using up loads of time but failing to find a solution to my problems. Sokolov's last move is outwardly surprising in that leaving yourself open to a discovered check can often be fatal. Here, however, attempts by Black to exploit this simply rebound. For example, 17...♗a3+? 18 ♔f1 ♗xb2 19 ♗h6 ♗xc3 20 ♗xg7 and Black can resign.

17...g6?

The immediate 17...♕c7 is more resilient, but White is still better after 18 ♗b3 ♕xh2 19 ♔f1!.

18 ♕f3 ♕c7 19 ♗b3 ♕xh2

Some would say suicidal, but what else?

20 ♖h1 ♕c7 21 ♔f1 ♕d8

The bishop on b3 points very menacingly at the f7 weakness and ties Black up in knots. The stark reality is that I have just played four pawn moves, followed by four queen moves, grabbing an irrelevant pawn before retreating back to base. Meanwhile Sokolov has been sensibly building an irresistible attack.

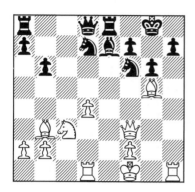

22 ♖e1

With the threat of ♘d5. I could have already resigned with quite a clear conscience, but given that it was my first ever game at the Hastings Premier, I was determined to make it to at least move 25!

22...♖f8 23 ♗a4 b5 24 ♗xb5 ♖b8 25 ♗xd7 ♕xd7 26 ♖xe7 ♕xe7 27 ♗xf6 ♕e6 28 d5 ♕a6+ 29 ♔g2 ♖b6 30 ♘e4 1-0

I remember watching this next game as it took place and very much admiring Black's play. For part of the game it superficially looks as though White has Black's uncontested bishop under lock and key, but this control proves to be temporary and a pleasing exchange sacrifice finally unleashes its untamed power.

Womacka-Harikrishna
Gibraltar Masters 2004
Ruy Lopez

1 e4 e5 2 ♘f3 ♘c6 3 ♗b5 ♘f6 4 0-0 ♘xe4 5 d4 ♘d6 6 ♗xc6

All main line theory at present, but for how much longer? In their 2000 world championship match Kasparov could make no impression on Kramnik's 'Berlin Wall' and in this game White is sure going to miss that bishop!

6...dxc6 7 dxe5 ♘f5 8 ♕xd8+ ♔xd8 9 ♘c3 ♗d7 10 h3 ♔c8 11 b3 b6 12 ♗b2 ♗e7 13 g4 ♘h4 14 ♘xh4 ♗xh4 15 f4

It should be said that White's lust to expand on the kingside is entirely logical given that he has the pawn majority here, but just watch those black bishops enjoy the open spaces.

15...f5! 16 exf6

Both 16 gxf5? ♗xf5 and 16 g5? (which could be answered by 16...h6!) are not what White is looking for.

16...gxf6!

Excellent and non-stereotyped play from the talented young Indian GM. The temptation is surely to capture with the bishop, but I like the pawn capture for two reasons. Firstly, Black doesn't allow White the chance to exchange bishops with ♘d1 or ♘a4, and secondly after the text move White has to be wary of Black striking at the white majority with either ...h5, ...f5 or both.

17 f5 h5 18 ♔g2?

I can understand White's eagerness to add support to his pawns with his king, but after this his majesty is at the mercy of Black's bishop on d7.

In hindsight I prefer the more direct 18 ♘e4. Then one plausible continuation is 18...hxg4 19 hxg4 ♖g8 20 ♘xf6 ♗xf6 21 ♗xf6 ♖xg4+ 22 ♔h2 ♔b7 23 ♖ad1 ♖f8 24 ♔h3 ♖gg8 25 ♖xd7 ♖xf6 26 ♖d4 ♖g5 27 ♖df4 ♖h6+ 28 ♔h4 ♖f6 29 ♖hf4 with a cute draw by repetition.

18...c5! 19 ♘d5 ♗c6

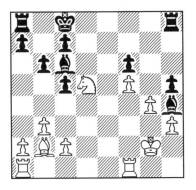

Finally the bishop announces its entry into the game.

20 c4

For the moment it looks as if White has successfully nullified Black's extra bishop, but it soon becomes apparent that this is not the case.

20...♔b7 21 ♖ae1!?

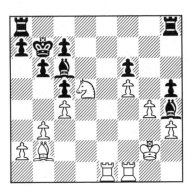

An imaginative offer of an exchange sacrifice, but actually this is the first indication that it's Black who is dictating events. Simply supporting the knight with 21 ♖ad1 allows 21...♖ae8! and White already has to deal with threats such as ...♖e2+ or ...♖e3.

21...♖ad8!

Black insists that he will be the one to give up the exchange.

21...♗xe1? 22 ♖xe1 is what White was after. Black's initiative dies once one of the bishop pair is exchanged and the kingside pawn majority coupled with the obvious weakness on f6 gives White more than sufficient compensation for the material deficit.

22 ♖e7 ♖xd5!

The bishop's path must be unblocked!

23 cxd5 ♗xd5+ 24 ♔h2

Or 24 ♔g1 hxg4 25 hxg4 ♗g3 with an imminent mate on h1.

24...hxg4 25 ♖f4?

A blunder in a difficult position. White must try 25 ♖g1.

25...g3+ 26 ♔g1 ♗g5! 0-1

The move ...♖xh3 will be decisive, the bishop on c6 having the final say.

Taming the bishop pair

We've already talked about how powerful the bishop pair can be (together a centralised pair can control 26 squares on an open board – only one less than the queen). However, on the flip side, more than any other piece the bishop needs its partner to display its full potential. This is simply because they control completely different squares and thus complement rather than reinforce each other – in other words there's no wasted firepower.

There are some recognised methods of trying to fight against the bishop pair, although you have to bear in mind that each position has to be judged on its own merits. Here's a brief summary of the options available:

1) Keep the position closed.

2) Restrict one of the bishop pair by putting pawns on the same colour.

3) Seek play on the colour complex of your remaining bishop.

4) Seek to exchange your remaining bishop for its opponent in the bishop pair. This idea may be especially success-ful if you exchange your opponent's 'good' bishop.

Concentrating on option '4' for the moment, one of the questions asked in Chapter 2 is especially relevant here: will a particular exchange have an impact upon the relative strengths and weak-nesses of the other pieces that remain on the board?

Most experts agree that the value of the bishop pair is very often greater than the sum of its individual components. As Jonathan Rowson writes in his very en-tertaining *The Seven Deadly Chess Sins*, 'What happens when you capture the opponent's bishop is not only that you remove one piece of value, but that you "weaken" the other bishop too'. Peter Wells expands on this, mentioning that pieces can easily 'shelter' from one bishop on the 32 squares that are out of its reach. So it seems logical that this exchange will help the player fighting the bishop pair.

Another factor that was touched upon in Chapter 2 is the control of a particular

colour complex. While the unopposed bishop of a bishop pair may well give its possessor control over a certain colour of squares (as seen in some of the exam-ples above), his opponent can hope to seek compensation on the other colour, where his extra knight may make a dif-ference. We've already seen a successful example of this idea in the game Bach-Schmall (page 60), where the initial part of White's overall strategy is to give Black the bishop pair. This possible con-trol is more often than not enhanced by the exchange of bishops, as witnessed in this somewhat clear-cut example, taken from one of my recent games.

Dannevig-Emms
Isle of Man 2003
Sicilian Defence

1 e4 c5 2 ♘f3 e6 3 b3 b6 4 d4 cxd4 5 ♘xd4 a6 6 ♗d3 ♗b7 7 0-0 d6 8 ♗b2 ♘f6 9 ♘d2 ♘bd7 10 f4 e5 11 ♘f5 g6 12 ♘e3 exf4 13 ♘d5 ♗g7 14 ♖xf4 ♗xd5 15 exd5 0-0 16 ♕f1 b5 17 c4 b4 18 ♗d4

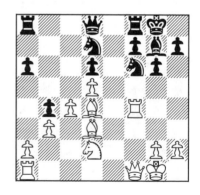

18...♘h5!

Typical anti-bishop pair strategy – Black forces the exchange of White's better bishop, even though there was certainly nothing wrong with Black's bishop on g7. In this example the control of the dark squares is clearly an important factor, and out of the remaining four minor pieces, White's bishop on d3 is certainly the odd one out.

19 ♗xg7 ♔xg7 20 ♖f2 ♘c5 21 ♖e1 ♘f6 22 ♖f4 ♖a7!

I figured that White's temporary kingside initiative could be extinguished with the exchange of one pair of rooks, thus the idea of ...♖e7.

23 ♗c2 ♖e7 24 ♖xe7 ♕xe7 25 ♕a1 ♖e8 26 ♘e4 ♘cxe4 27 ♖xe4 ♕a7+ 28 ♔f1 ♖xe4 29 ♗xe4 ♕e3 30 ♗f3 a5

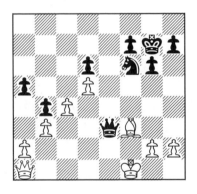

The situation has clarified somewhat and we arrive at an admittedly very lopsided example of a queen and knight working together in perfect harmony against a queen and bishop. (I don't intend to discuss John Watson's persuasive argument in *Secrets of Modern Chess Strategy* that in general the superiority of queen and knight over queen and bishop in the endgame is somewhat a fallacy.)

I'm not sure that I played the best moves from now on, but such is Black's superiority here that a few second best

moves is unlikely to change the assessment of a clear advantage to Black.

31 ♕b2 ♕f4 32 h3 h5 33 ♔f2 ♔f8 34 ♕e2 ♕h4+ 35 ♔g1 ♘d7 36 ♕f2 ♕d8!

It's even worth allowing White's queen some activity. In the long run Black has more winning chances with the queens on the board.

37 ♕a7 ♔g7 38 ♔f2 ♘c5! 39 ♔e2 a4! 40 bxa4 ♕f6 41 ♕b6 ♕e5+! 42 ♔f2 ♕d4+

Regaining the pawn with check as 43 ♔g3 loses to 43...♘e4+.

43 ♔f1 ♕a1+ 44 ♔f2 ♕xa2+ 45 ♔g3 ♕xc4 46 ♕xd6 ♕c3

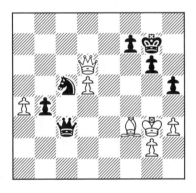

Both sides have passed pawns but Black's b-pawn will be the decisive runner. Notice that White's bishop on f3 hasn't been much more than a spectator for a good many moves.

47 ♕b8 b3 48 h4

Or 48 d6 b2 and there is no good defence to ...♕e1+.

48...b2 49 ♔h2 ♘d7 50 ♕b7 ♘e5 0-1

Now to two games that both reach the same position after White's 9th move. In the first game White successfully carries out the plan of exchanging one of the bishop pair, while in the second Black directly prevents this option and finally the bishop pair is successful.

Wells-Chandler
British League 1997
Sicilian Defence

1 e4 c5 2 ♘f3 ♘c6 3 ♗b5 g6

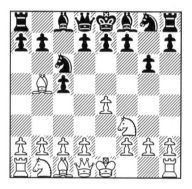

4 ♗xc6

Although this move seems to be very popular these days, especially at the highest levels, for me it makes an unusual impression to exchange on c6 so early and without provocation. In fact we shall see that White has a concrete reason for playing like this, but even so I was still very comforted to read Kramnik's comments in *New In Chess*: 'This move I actually find quite strange. It's amazing that after this move White can fight for an advantage, and he often does so successfully. For me there's no logic in the move. Nobody's attacking the bishop and it looks as if you give up the bishop for the knight for no reason at all. Still White pretends to be better. Strange but true.' Perhaps the popularity of 4 ♗xc6 is simply down to fashion, and by

the time this book comes out, everyone will be playing the more obvious 4 0-0 again!

4...dxc6

After the recapture chosen in the game Black has easy development but his pawn structure is compromised to the effect that it's quite immobile and offers little chance of pawn breaks.

In many ways Black would prefer to capture with 4...bxc6. He captures towards the centre and has a more mobile pawn mass (one long-term plan is ...d7-d6, ...e7-e5 and the pawn break ...f7-f5). However, it seems that this recapture suffers from specific problems and not many strong players are willing to go down these lines (in my latest *TWIC* database 4...dxc6 appears with more than twice the frequency of 4...bxc6). The main disadvantage of playing 4...bxc6 as Black is that easy development is a problem and White tries to exploit this by opening the centre. I don't want to delve too deeply into this one particular opening line, but after 5 0-0 ♗g7 6 ♖e1!

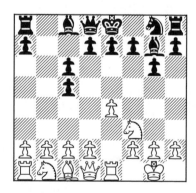

here is a brief summary of why this line is, at the moment at least, causing a few headaches for Black:

a) 6...♘f6 (Black tries to develop

quickly) 7 e5! ♘d5 8 c4! ♘c7 9 d4 cxd4 10 ♕xd4 0-0 11 ♕h4 d6 12 ♗h6 ♘e6 13 ♘c3 with a very strong position for White, Kasparov-Salov, Dortmund 1992. It was games like this that put many Black players off 4 ...bxc6.

b) 6...♘h6!? 7 c3 0-0 8 d4 cxd4 9 cxd4 f6!? followed by ...♘f7 and ...d7-d6 is an imaginative way for Black to solve his developmental problems and has been tried by a few strong GMs. One can understand a reluctance to play like this but Black is probably only a little worse.

c) 6...d6 7 e5! is annoying, as White threatens to saddle Black with horrible weaknesses by e5xd6. However, 7...d5, leaving c5 vulnerable, is also not ideal for Black.

d) 6...e5 seems very logical. As I mentioned before, Black wants to follow up with ...d6, ...♘e7, ...0-0 and eventually prepare ...f5. Again, despite fighting against the bishop pair, White should attempt to open up the position in the centre; for example, 7 c3! ♘e7 8 d4! cxd4 9 cxd4 exd4 10 ♘xd4 0-0 11 ♘c3. To a certain extent Black's position looks quite dynamic, but there are problems: the d7-c6 pawn cluster could prove to be weak and the c8-bishop may find it difficult to find a useful role. Theory states that White has some advantage here but, despite what I said above, I'm not so sure. To me it does look like the sort of position in which a few accurate moves would give Black a very playable position.

5 d3 ♗g7 6 h3

With Black's static pawn structure but easy development, White opts for a completely different strategy to that after 4...bxc6. Peter Wells calls this 'closure

and restriction'. White's previous move prevents both ...♘f6-g4 and ...♗g4, and already the future of the c8-bishop looks uncertain.

6...♘f6 7 ♘c3 ♘d7 8 ♗e3! e5 9 ♕d2!

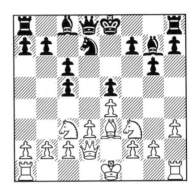

White prepares to put into practice the main idea that we chatted about in the introduction: exchanging off one of the bishop pair. It's a fair question to ask 'why does White want to force this exchange?' After all, the bishop on g7 is blocked by the pawn on e5 and it certainly doesn't look any more powerful than White's bishop on e3. However, this argument fails to take into consideration the long-term effects in this position. For one thing, the bishop on g7 is required to cover the weakened dark squares in Black's camp. Remember that with the exchange of these bishops White has two minor pieces that can control dark squares while Black has only one. Another point is that at some stage the position could well open up, and White wants to avoid leaving Black with the bishop pair in this situation.

9...♕e7

We'll check out 9...h6 in the next game.

10 ♗h6! ♗xh6 11 ♕xh6 f6 12 ♘d2!

Preparing the typical f2-f4 break.

12...♘f8 13 f4 ♘e6?!

With this move Black keeps a pawn on e5, but it will be isolated and vulnerable without Black having any obvious compensation.

Instead Black should give up the centre with 13...exf4. Following 14 ♕xf4 ♘e6 15 ♕f2 Black's knight eyes the d4-square and he has reasonable chances to equalise, although in Wells's words: 'It is difficult to escape the fact that of the four minor pieces it is most problematic to envisage exciting career prospects for the bishop.'

14 fxe5 fxe5 15 ♘e2!

Covering both d4 and f4 in case of occupation by the black knight.

15...♗d7 16 0-0 0-0-0 17 ♘c4

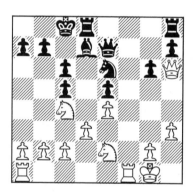

Eyeing the weak e5-pawn and threatening ♖f7!. White's opening has been a success: he has inflicted structural weaknesses on his opponent, swapped off one of the bishop pair and left the other bishop without a good future – all good, classic 'anti-bishop pair' strategy. Wells eventually manages to convert his obvious superiority – I'll give the rest of the game without notes.

17...♗e8 18 ♖f2 ♘c7 19 a4 ♘a6 20 ♖af1 ♘b4 21 ♘c1 ♖g8 22 ♕e3 b5 23 ♘a3 ♘a6 24 ♘b3 g5 25 ♖f5 g4 26 ♕g3 ♗d7 27 ♖f7 ♕d6 28 ♖1f6 gxh3 29 ♕e3 ♖xg2+ 30 ♔h1 ♗e6 31 axb5 ♖dg8 32 ♘c4 ♕d8 33 ♖xe6 ♖g1+ 34 ♔h2 ♖8g2+ 35 ♔xh3 ♖h2+ 36 ♔xh2 1-0

Ponomariov-Kramnik
Linares 2003
Sicilian Defence

1 e4 c5 2 ♘f3 ♘c6 3 ♗b5 g6 4 ♗xc6 dxc6 5 d3 ♗g7 6 h3 ♘f6 7 ♘c3 ♘d7 8 ♗e3 e5 9 ♕d2 h6!?

Kramnik writes of this move: '...I think that the text move is one of the most critical tests for White's set-up in this line, preventing the bishop from coming to h6. The continuation of the black plan is quite simple: he wants to put the knight on d4 with ...♕e7, ...♘f8-e6-d4. And White has to act quickly to stop it, because if Black succeeds he will simply be better.'

10 0-0 ♕e7 11 a3

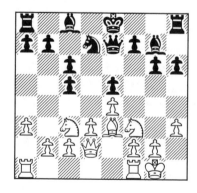

Ponomariov opts to play on the queenside, a plan that Kramnik manages to defuse. In his opinion it's probably better for White to play for f2-f4 as in the previous game. Even so, after say 11 ♘h2 ♘f8 12 f4 exf4! 13 ♖xf4 ♘e6 14 ♖f2 ♘d4 15 ♖af1 ♗e6 16 b3 0-0-0 (as in Pikula-Kovacevic, Yugoslavia 2002) Black's bishop on g7 covers some important squares and Black is certainly better off than in the game Wells-Chandler.

11...♘f8 12 b4 ♘e6 13 ♘a4

Somewhat paradoxically, White offers Black the chance to undouble his c-pawns. However, this would be at a cost of giving White a half-open a-file and immediate threats of ♘a4-b6. Kramnik finds a clever way round this plan.

13...b6! 14 ♘h2

Kramnik's idea was to meet 14 bxc5 with 14...b5! 15 ♘c3 f5! 16 exf5 gxf5 when the threat of ...f5-f4 causes White problems.

14...f5

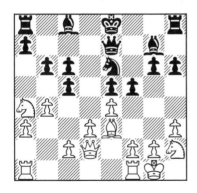

15 f3?

After this move White accepts that he is worse and Black takes over the initiative in no uncertain terms. Kramnik was much more concerned about the variation 15 exf5 gxf5 16 f4! exf4 17 ♗xf4 ♗xa1 18 ♖xa1 ♖g8 19 ♖e1, when White has finally eliminated that dark-squared

bishop, albeit for a rook. Kramnik goes on to say: '...objectively Black should be fine, but the position is not easy to play with the knight coming to f3 and the vulnerability of the black squares.'

15...f4 16 ♗f2 h5!

Black has an obvious plan of attack on the kingside.

17 bxc5 b5 18 ♘b2 g5

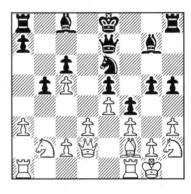

19 d4?

Sensing impending problems on the kingside with ...g5-g4, Ponomariov panics somewhat, and opens up the position to Black's advantage. As an improvement Kramnik gives 19 a4 g4! (the only consistent follow-up to Black's previous moves) 20 fxg4 hxg4 21 ♘xg4 ♘g5 with an obviously dangerous attack on the kingside. But as Kramnik points out, '...it's not so easy to mate, especially when the computer starts to defend.'

19...exd4 20 ♘d3 ♘xc5 21 ♘xc5 ♕xc5 22 ♖fd1 ♗e6 23 ♕b4

23 ♗xd4 ♗xd4+ 24 ♕xd4 ♕xd4+ 25 ♖xd4 ♔e7 is a very unpleasant ending for White. Black has a simple plan of exchanging rooks on the d-file and simply pushing the queenside pawns. In this situation the knight on h2 is a very poor piece.

23...♕b6!

Black wishes to keep the pair of bishops, whose influence is growing move by move. 23...♕xb4 24 axb4 d3 25 cxd3! ♗xa1 26 ♖xa1 (Kramnik) is obviously better for Black but there is no clear way to win.

24 a4

24 ♗xd4 ♗xd4+ 25 ♕xd4 (25 ♖xd4?? c5!) 25...♕xd4+ 26 ♖xd4 ♔e7 reaches the note to White's 23rd move.

24...c5 25 ♕xb5+ ♕xb5 26 axb5 ♔f7 27 ♖a5 ♖hb8 28 ♘f1

28 ♖da1 d3! 29 ♖xa7+ ♔g6 30 ♖xg7+ ♔xg7 31 ♖xa8 dxc2! 32 ♖xb8 (32 ♖a1 ♖xb5) 32...c1♕+ 33 ♘f1 ♗c4 (Kramnik) is very similar to the game continuation.

28...♗e5 29 ♖da1 d3!

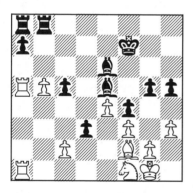

Black's decision on move nine now seems to be paying great dividends. Just compare the activity of the minor pieces. On the other hand, 29...d3 only works due to concrete reasons, well calculated by Kramnik.

30 ♖xa7+ ♔f6! 31 ♖xa8 ♖xa8 32 ♖xa8

32 ♖c1 loses to 32...♗b2; while 32 ♖d1 dxc2 33 ♖c1 ♗b3 34 ♘d2 c4 35 ♘xc4 ♖a1 is also winning for Black.

32...dxc2

The point – promotion to a queen cannot be prevented and White is totally lost.

33 ♖f8+ ♔g7 34 ♖e8 ♔f7 35 ♖f8+!?

After the similar 35 ♖e7+ Black can capture: 35...♔xe7 36 ♗xc5+ ♗d6!.

35...♔g6 36 ♖e8 ♗c4! 37 ♖xe5 c1♕ 38 ♖xc5 ♕xf1+ 39 ♔h2 ♕xf2 40 ♖xc4 g4 0-1

Black mates after 41 hxg4 hxg4 42 fxg4 f3 and ...♕g2.

A step backwards

It's been said many times before that it's very easy to overlook a retreating move and, more specifically, a knight retreat. The psychology of this common problem is quite easy to understand – most chess players are much keener to look forwards rather than backwards, and many would agree that in general the knight is the most difficult piece to handle.

One of the most famous blunders of all time occurred through an inability to spot a knight retreat, and the victim was none other than ex-world champion Anatoly Karpov.

Karpov-Kasparov
World Ch'ship (game 11) Seville 1987

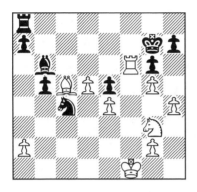

35 ♗f2 keeps a clear edge in this endgame. Instead Karpov ventured with
35 ♖c6??

only to be hit by
35...♘a5!

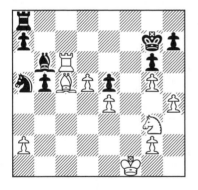

after which Kasparov won the exchange and later the game. In the end Kasparov only managed to retain his title by winning the final game to draw the match 12-12, so it could be said that this knight retreat altered the history of chess!

To be fair to Karpov, it's not often he misses a knight retreat. The following two examples redress the balance somewhat.

Karpov-Spassky
9th match game, Leningrad 1974

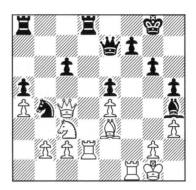

This case is almost as famous as the previous example and is often used to show Karpov's mastery of positional play. White already has a very pleasant position, but Karpov's non-stereotyped play makes it look like a forced win for White.
24 ♘b1!

The knight was clearly restricted on c3 and this move begins a very effective reorganisation of the white pieces. White plans to kick away the black knight with c2-c3, followed by ♖e2 and a knight manoeuvre to the kingside with ♘d2-f3, where it hits the bishop on h4 and eyes the weakened dark squares. There was little Spassky could do to counter this plan.
24...♕b7 25 ♔h2

Typical Karpov prophylaxis, preventing any thoughts of ...♗g3.
25...♔g7 26 c3 ♘a6

Now this knight has no future and White will soon be in a 'power play' situation.
27 ♖e2!

Showing a very deep appreciation of the position. Karpov gives up the d-file for the moment to augment the knight manoeuvre, but correctly judges that Black cannot make any use of it. In fact, in a few moves time it's back in White's possession.

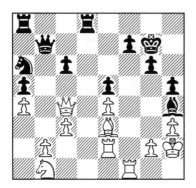

27...♖f8 28 ♘d2 ♗d8 29 ♘f3 f6 30 ♖d2 ♗e7 31 ♕e6! ♖ad8 32 ♖xd8 ♗xd8

The alternative 32...♖xd8 allows the simple response 33 ♘xe5! fxe5 34 ♖f7+ and wins.

33 ♖d1 ♘b8 34 ♗c5 ♖h8

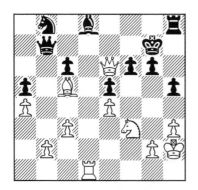

35 ♖xd8! 1-0

35...♖xd8 36 ♗e7 is crushing; for example, 36...♖e8 37 ♕xf6+ ♔h7 38 ♕f7+ ♔h6 39 ♗g5 mate.

This following snippet involving Kar-

pov is not as well known as the previous example.

Korchnoi-Karpov
World Ch'ship (game 13), Baguio 1978

Black seems to be under some heavy pressure on the queenside, but Karpov's use of the knight on c7 is exemplary.

26...b5!

What's this?

27 ♕b3 ♘a8!

Now we see the idea! Black plans to block the c-file and thus shield the weak c6-pawn with ...♘b6-c4. White can do little to stop this.

28 a4 bxa4 29 ♕xa4 ♘b6 30 ♕b3 ♖b8 31 ♘f4 ♘c4

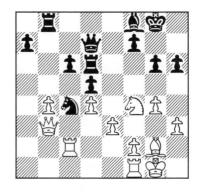

and Black has fully equalised.

The late Tony Miles had a particularly good grasp of the intricacies of the knight retreat. I first came across the following example when I was looking for moves for 'the deep and mysterious' chapter of my book *The Most Amazing Chess Moves of All Time*. I can't resist showing it again – it's probably the knight retreat against which all others should be measured.

Miles-Makarichev
Oslo 1984

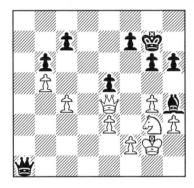

White's centralised queen gives him an advantage, but it seems very difficult to make progress. If White goes after the c-pawn with 37 ♕c6 then the simple 37...♗xg3 38 ♔xg3 ♕g1+ is sufficient for Black, while 37 ♘e2? is answered by 37...♕e1!. Miles's solution is quite mind-boggling on first sight. I remember wondering how many other GMs would be able to come up with such a move.

37 ♘h1!!

This is a case of a piece looking terrible but performing a concrete role in a position. The h1-square is not the first place a knight would choose to go, but just for this position it's in the perfect location! The logic is that White's only

weak point (the f2-pawn) is now securely protected. In fact the white king and knight easily rebuff any attack from black's queen and bishop, leaving the white queen free to attack Black's weaknesses (the c7-pawn in particular).

Superficially the knight is dominated by the bishop on h4, but I still believe it's the better piece! Or at least White's queen and knight work better than Black's queen and bishop, so it's worth retaining this piece. And as we see, Black isn't able to keep the knight in the corner for such a long time.

37...♕b2

Black gives up the c7-pawn, a sure indication that his position is worse than it looks. Black can keep the pawn but only at a cost of accepting complete passivity after 37...♗f6 38 ♕c6 ♕a7 39 ♘g3! ♗h4 40 ♘e4. Lines like this demonstrate why Miles was so keen to keep the knight at any cost.

38 ♕c6 ♕b1 39 ♕xc7 ♕e4+ 40 ♔h2 h5 41 ♕c6 ♕c2

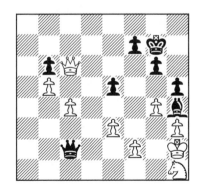

42 gxh5!

Weaker is 42 ♔g2 ♗g5 43 ♕d5 h4! 44 ♕xe5+ ♗f6 (Miles), when White has trouble winning because it's difficult to get the knight into the game. After the text move 42...♗xf2 loses to 43 ♕g2 and Miles is able to convert his advantage.

42...♕f5 43 ♕g2 ♕xh5 44 c5! bxc5 45 b6 ♕d1 46 ♕c6! ♗e7 47 ♘g3 c4 48 b7 ♗d6 49 ♘e4 ♗b8 50 ♕c8 ♕f3 51 ♕xb8 ♕xe4 52 ♕c7 ♕f3 53 ♔g1 ♕d1+ 54 ♔g2 ♕d5+ 55 ♔g3 1-0

This second example involving Tony Miles really appealed to me. It's not often that one is allowed to play three consecutive knight retreats to end up in the corner of the board!

Toth-Miles
Reggio Emilia 1984

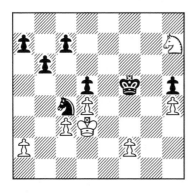

Black's target is White's vulnerable h4-pawn, so...

37...♘d6! 38 f3 ♘f7! 39 ♔e3 ♘h8!!

A move very much for the spectators!

40 ♘g5

Or 40 ♔f2 ♘g6 41 ♔g3 ♘f4 (threatening ...♘e2+) 42 ♔f2 ♘e6!, when six consecutive knight moves have left White's own knight without an escape square.

40...♘g6

The h-pawn drops off and Black wins easily.

41 ♘h3 c6 42 ♘f2 ♘xh4 43 ♘d3 ♘g6 44 ♘b4 ♘e7 45 ♔f2 a5 46 ♘d3 ♘g6 47 ♔g3 ♘f4! 48 ♘e5

48 ♘xf4 loses to 48...h4+!.

48...♘e2+ 49 ♔h4 ♘xc3 50 ♘xc6 ♘xa2 51 ♘e7+ ♔e6 0-1

My interest in this subject of knight retreats was rekindled to some extent after a painful experience in a very recent game.

Rowson-Emms
Gibraltar 2004

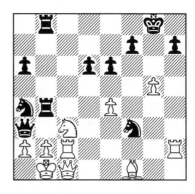

I had just captured a pawn with ...♘(e5)xf3 and I was expecting Jonathan to resign in a couple of moves. In fact, after the game continuation 32 ♖hf2?

♘d4 no one would argue if White threw in the towel. Unfortunately for me, Jonathan played a few more desperate moves and I somehow managed to convert a winning position into a lost one. I'll leave that story for another time (on second thoughts, perhaps I won't – those interested will find the game on *TWIC* database!).

While I was inputting my game into ChessBase and letting Fritz find an enormous number of wins for Black, I (or perhaps Fritz – I can't remember exactly) did find an amazing resource for White that Jonathan and myself either failed to consider or rejected during the game.

The point is that White can actually stay in the game after **32 ♔a1!**. During the game I rejected this as a possibility for White in view of **32...♘xb2** 33 ♖xb2? ♘xh2, when Black wins easily, but White has the much stronger move in **33 ♘b1!!**.

Now I can't honestly remember if I spotted this idea or not during the game. It's even possible that I did see this but rejected it because of 33...♕xa2+?? 34 ♔xa2 ♖a4+, missing 35 ♘a3(!). In any case, after 33 ♘b1!! Black doesn't actu-

ally have a totally convincing reply, for example:

a) 33...♕a5 34 ♖c8+ (perhaps it's this I missed) 34...♖xc8 35 ♕xc8+ ♔g7 36 ♕c3+ ♕e5 37 ♖xb2 and White is better.

b) 33...♘d3! (I'm not sure I would have seen this; Fritz, of course has no problems spotting knight retreats!) 34 ♘xa3 ♘xc1 35 ♖h3 ♘xg5 36 ♖g3 f6 37 ♖xc1 ♖xe4 38 ♗xa6 with a very unclear endgame.

Looking back at the original position, it somehow seems unfair that White has a defence that works, but this example does go some way to showing how good a knight can be protecting its king. Have you ever tried checkmating with queen and king versus knight and king in blitz – it's not that easy! I even found an example on my database of a well-known grandmaster failing to win this position in a competitive game (I'm sure time was a big factor).

The following example appealed to me in the way White's king's knight manages to find the home of its partner very early on in the game. Despite this, White's play does have a cast-iron logic to it.

De Haan-Ligterink
Dutch League, Amsterdam 2000
Queen's Indian Defence

1 d4 ♘f6 2 c4 e6 3 ♘f3 b6 4 a3 ♗a6 5 ♕c2 ♗b7 6 ♘c3 c5 7 dxc5 bxc5 8 ♗f4 ♗e7 9 ♖d1 d6?

This leads Black to some surprising problems. Black should have left this pawn on d7 for the time being and simply played 9...0-0.

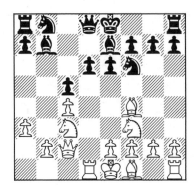

10 ♘b5!

This rather unsubtle attack on d6 is actually very difficult to meet.

10...♘e4

I guess Black was pinning his hopes on this move, but White has a very effective reply.

11 ♘d2!

The point; the knight on e4 comes under fire and Black's position is already on the verge of collapsing.

11...♘f6!

The most resilient defence is a knight retreat, but the fun is only just starting!

12 ♘b1!

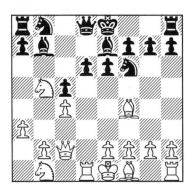

Three knight retreats in a row again! The knight vacates the d-file to renew the attack on d6, the circuit of ♘g1-f3-d2-b1 making quite a striking impression. Now Black is forced to give up the d6-pawn.

12...♗e4

12...♘e4 13 ♘1c3! is the reason why White chose 12 ♘b1! over, say, 12 ♘b3.

13 ♕c1 ♗xb1 14 ♕xb1

A couple of pieces have been exchanged but Black has not managed to solve the main problem: the d6-pawn is going to drop off.

14...0-0 15 ♗xd6 ♗xd6 16 ♖xd6 ♕e7 17 ♖d1

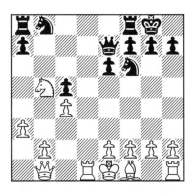

White is a pawn up and Black's slight lead in development provides insufficient compensation. White's cheeky opening idea has worked a treat!

17...♘c6 18 e3 ♖ab8 19 ♗e2 a6 20 ♘c3 ♖b3 21 ♕c2 ♖fb8 22 ♖b1 ♕c7 23 0-0 ♕b6 24 ♖fd1 ♖xb2?

This loses to a back rank tactic.

25 ♖xb2 ♕xb2 26 ♕xb2 ♖xb2 27 ♗f3! 1-0

Exercises

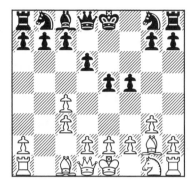

Exercise 3.1 White to play

This position arises after the opening moves **1 c4 e5 2 ♘c3 ♗b4** (Black is not afraid to give up the bishop pair if it means gaining time or inflicting damage on White's pawn structure) **3 g3 ♗xc3 4 bxc3 d6 5 ♗g2 f5**. Can you spot a rather drastic way for White to make use of his unopposed bishop on c1?

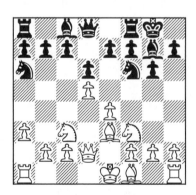

Exercise 3.2 White to play

This position arose after the opening sequence **1 e4 d6 2 d4 g6 3 ♘f3 ♗g7 4 ♘c3 ♘f6 5 ♗e3 0-0 6 ♕d2 ♘c6 7 d5 ♘b4 8 a3 ♘a6**. Can you see a good idea for White here?

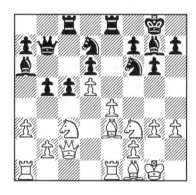

Exercise 3.3 White to play

White obviously has some pressure on the kingside in this position. Can you see how this can be increased?

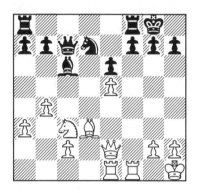

Exercise 3.4 Black to play

White has just played the move ♗g2-f1. Can you suggest a good plan of action for Black?

CHAPTER FOUR

Dancing Queens

The queen is by far the most powerful piece on the chessboard. It displays the combined power of the rook and bishop and covers an amazing 27 squares from the centre of an open board. However, the queen is also a very difficult piece to handle. Part of the reason for this is that its high value actually makes it vulnerable. When attacked by pieces of lower value the queen virtually always has to move out of the way and of course this loses time. Beginners have problems using the queen effectively; they often try to win the game by using the queen alone and usually wind up miles behind in development as their queen is pushed from pillar to post.

In this chapter I would like to take a look at some features of the queen, one or two of which I believe haven't been covered at length before.

Queen power

In this section I would like to take a brief look at how a queen fares against other pieces configurations of roughly similar value in different positions. The first thing that should be mentioned is that the queen is a very powerful attacking piece. Its mobility means that it can attack weaknesses quickly and it is particularly effective against a weakened king, when it can gain much time with continued checking and mating threats. Queens are less happy when having to defend (they are actually quite bad at this) or performing mundane tasks such as blocking a passed pawn or protecting a weakness (this is often a huge waste of firepower).

I find this first example particularly instructive in that Black seems to have more than enough material compensation, but it's still the queen that triumphs in the end.

Ivanchuk-Adams
Linares 2002

It was tempting to annotate the moves leading up to this position because it was such an eventful game, but I resisted as it's not strictly to do with our theme. Suffice to say that Mickey Adams probably should have played a move earlier which lead to a perpetual check, although in fairness it was very difficult to work out all the consequences of the complications.

Now in this position, despite battling against rook, knight and bishop, the queen still has the advantage. This is in some way due to its activity but more importantly it's down to Black's very open king position plus the obvious targets that the queen can attack. Although objectively Black's isn't doing terribly badly, this type of position is always difficult to defend practically because of the number of checks, attacks and double attacks that Black has to watch out for. It's unsurprising that in practical play Black fails to find the most stubborn defence.

25 ♕c5+ ♔d7 26 ♕d4+

Immediately picking up a pawn.

26...♔e7 27 ♕xg7

After this capture the material count (queen and two pawns for rook, bishop and knight) is roughly level, but White still keeps a plus due to the active queen and weak black king.

27...bxa4?

It's tempting to grab a pawn, but according to Ivanchuk Black should consolidate on the queenside with 27...♗d5!

28 ♕xh7 ♖h8 29 ♕f5 c6. In this case it would be difficult for White to exploit his majority on the kingside, as the pawns are split and thus somewhat weak.

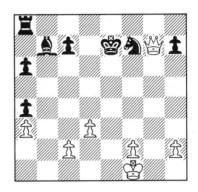

28 ♕c3!

Correctly judging that it's more important to attack the queenside pawns.

28...♔d7 29 ♕d4+ ♘d6 30 ♕xa4+ ♔e6 31 ♕g4+ ♘f5 32 ♕c4+

32...♗d5?

Black decides to give up his c-pawn rather than his h-pawn, which he hopes will generate some counterplay in the long run. However, this is a mistake in a very difficult position, after which White obtains a decisive advantage.

Following 32...♔d7! 33 ♕f7+ ♘e7 34 ♕xh7 ♖f8 (Ivanchuk) Black still keeps slim drawing chances.

33 ♕xc7

Now the advance of White's connected passed pawns on the c- and d-files will prove to be decisive.

33...h5 34 c4 ♗h1 35 f4

Threatening ♕e5+.

35...♖f8 36 ♕b6+

The immediate 36 d4 ♔f6 37 d5 (Ivanchuk) is also very strong.

36...♔f7 37 ♕a7+ ♘e7 38 ♕xa6 ♖b8 39 d4 ♖b1+ 40 ♔e2 ♖b2+ 41 ♔d3 ♖b3+

Or 41...♖xh2 42 d5 ♗f3 43 ♕e6+ ♔e8 44 d6 ♖e2 45 ♕f6 ♘c6 46 c5 ♖e1 47 ♕g7 followed by ♕g8+, ♕f7+, ♕c7+ and d7+.

42 ♔d2 ♖h3 43 d5 ♖xh2+ 44 ♔d3

44...♘xd5

There is nothing better – the pawns are simply too strong.

45 cxd5 ♗xd5 46 f5 ♖a2 47 ♕a7+ ♔f6 48 ♕d4+ ♔g5 49 ♕xd5 ♖xa3+ 50 ♔e4 1-0

In the following example the queen is battling against two rooks – a very common scenario. Here the queen again has the upper hand due to the weakness of the opposing king.

De Vreugt-Gulko
Wijk aan Zee 2001

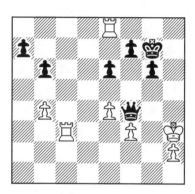

43...♕d2! 44 ♖a3 ♕f2!

An ideal place for the queen, which now hits both f3 and h2 and severely restricts White's king. It's instructive to see just how menacing the attack becomes when Black's king and pawns join forces to help the queen.

45 ♖e7 g5

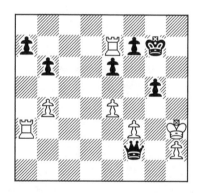

46 ♖exa7

Nominally White is material ahead but it's Black who has the winning position.

46...♔g6

Already threatening 47...♔h5 48 ♖xf7 ♕f1+ 49 ♔g3 ♕g1+ 50 ♔h3 g4+ 51 fxg4+ ♕xg4 mate. White has only one defence.

47 ♖a8 f5! 48 ♖g8+ ♔h6

But not 48...♔f6? 49 e5+! ♔xe5 50 ♖xg5 (Gulko), when White has chances of surviving.

49 exf5 exf5 50 b5

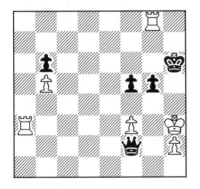

Now if it were White's move, Black would be winning easily, so Gulko employs a neat triangulation with his king (these don't have to be reserved only for pawn endings!).

50...♔h5!

Note that 50...♕f1+ 51 ♔g3 f4+? 52 ♔g4 ♕g1+ 53 ♔f5! (Gulko) allows White to escape and suddenly gives him counterplay. The key point is that 53...♕c5+ 54 ♔f6 ♕d6+ 55 ♔f7 ♕xa3?? allows mate in one with 56 ♖h8.

51 ♖h8+ ♔g6 52 ♖g8+ ♔h6!

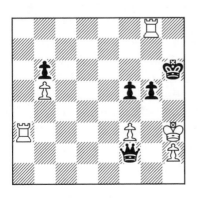

53 ♖h8+

All other moves lose instantly, for example:

a) 53 ♖ga8 (now g4 isn't covered so it's forced mate) 53...♕f1+ 54 ♔g3 ♕g1+ 55 ♔h3 g4+ 56 fxg4 ♕xg4 mate.

b) 53 ♖b3 ♕a2! skewers the rooks and wins one of them.

c) 53 ♖c3 allows a queen fork after 53...♕f1+ 54 ♔g3 ♕e1+.

53...♔g7 54 ♖ha8

Or 54 ♖c8 ♕f1+ 55 ♔g3 ♕g1+ 56 ♔h3 g4+ 57 ♔h4 ♕xh2+ 58 ♔g5 ♕h6+ 59 ♔xf5 ♕f6+ 60 ♔xg4 ♕e6+ and ...♕xc8.

54...♕f1+ 55 ♔g3 ♕g1+ 56 ♔h3 ♕f1+ 57 ♔g3 ♕g1+ 58 ♔h3 g4+! 59 ♔h4 gxf3

60 h3

White has to prevent ...♕g4 mate. After 60 ♖3a7+ ♔f6 61 ♖f8+ ♔e6 62 ♖e8+ ♔d6 63 ♖d8+ ♔c5 64 ♖c8+ ♔xb5 the checks run out.

60...♕e1+ 61 ♔g5 ♕e7+ 62 ♔h5

Black also wins after 62 ♔xf5 f2 63 ♖a1 f1♕+ 64 ♖xf1 ♕f6+.

62...♕f7+ 63 ♔g5 f2 64 ♖f3 ♕e7+ 0-1

65 ♔h5 ♕e2 66 ♖aa3 f1♕ is winning for Black.

When battling against two rooks, the queen often works very well with advanced passed pawns. Often the queen and pawn can reduce the rooks to a very passive role.

Miles-Ljubojevic
Linares 1985

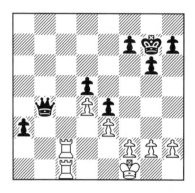

In this position White's king is safe enough, at least for the moment, but what sways the balance decisively in Black's favour is the power of the passed pawn on a3. Together this duo can virtually paralyse the rook pair.

33...♕b3 34 ♖c7

34 ♖d2 a2 35 ♖a1 ♕b1+ 36 ♖d1 ♕b2 leave the white rooks even more passively placed than in the game. Black's plan to win would be to steadily advance on the kingside, as in the game.

34...a2 35 ♖a7 ♕b2 36 ♖e1 g5 37 g3 ♕b1 38 ♖a8

White's king cannot approach. 38 ♔e2 is very rudely met by 38...♕d3 mate!

38...♔g6 39 h3 f5

Black's plan is to create an entry square for his king on the kingside. There is very little that White can do against this in the long term.

40 ♖a6+ ♔h5 41 ♖a8 h6

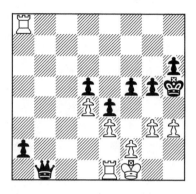

42 ♖a7

Against the more resilient 42 ♖a5! Ljubojevic shows a very pleasing way for Black to end White resistance: 42...♕d3+ (I should admit that the prosaic 42...f4 43 exf4 gxf4 44 ♖xd5+ ♔g6 45 ♖a5 fxg3 also wins) 43 ♖e2 (43 ♔g2 ♕d2 forks the rooks) 43...♕d1+ 44 ♖e1 ♕b1! (I really like this idea; just as in the previous example a nice triangulation – this time by the queen – puts White in zugzwang) 45 ♖a3 and now Black breaks through with 45...f4! as in the game.

42...f4 43 exf4

White can also die a slower death with 43 ♖a8, a defensive try not mentioned by Ljubojevic. Now one way to win involves totally paralysing White with 43...f3 followed by a king march to the queenside; for example, 44 ♖a7 (44 ♖a6 loses to 44...♕b5+) 44...♔g6 45 ♖a8 ♔f6 46 ♖a7 ♔e6 47 g4 ♔d6 48 ♖a5 ♔c6 49 ♖c5+ (49 ♖a8 ♔b7 and the rook runs out of squares, White losing after 50 ♖a5 ♔b8! 51 ♖a3 ♕b5+ 52 ♔g1 ♕b4) 49...♔b6 50 ♖cc1 ♕b2 51 ♖ed1 ♔b5 52 ♖e1 ♔b4 53 ♖ed1 ♔a3 54 ♖e1 ♕b5+ 55 ♔g1 ♔b2 56 ♖cd1 ♕d3! 57 ♖a1 ♕b1! 58 ♖axb1+ axb1♕ 59 ♖xb1+ ♔xb1, when finally the king and pawn ending is winning for Black.

43...gxf4 44 gxf4 ♔h4 45 ♖a3

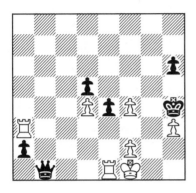

45...h5

This is good enough, but 45...e3! is a sweeter way to win: 46 fxe3 ♕b2 47 ♖a8 ♔g3 and White is getting mated.

46 f5 ♔g5 47 ♖a5 ♕d3+ 48 ♖e2 ♕d1+ 49 ♖e1 ♕b1!

Again Black uses the zugzwang theme.

50 ♖a8

Or 50 h4+ ♔f6.

50...♔xf5 51 ♖f8+ ♔g5 52 ♖a8 ♔h4 53 ♖a3 ♕b2 54 ♖a8 ♔xh3 55 ♔g1 ♕b1 56 ♖a3+ ♔g4 57 ♖f1 h4 58 ♖a8 h3 0-1

As I mentioned earlier, the queen is far less happy in a defensive role and this fact is evident in the following two examples where, despite battling against just a rook and minor piece, the queen finds it tough going.

Solozhenkin-Semkov
Berga 1992
Semi-Slav Defence

1 d4 d5 2 c4 e6 3 ♘f3 c6 4 e3 ♘f6 5 ♘c3 ♘bd7 6 ♗d3 ♗e7 7 0-0 0-0 8 ♕e2 dxc4 9 ♗xc4 b5 10 ♗d3 b4 11

♘e4 c5 12 ♘xf6+ ♘xf6 13 dxc5 ♗b7 14 e4 ♘d7 15 c6 ♗xc6 16 ♖d1 ♕b6 17 ♗e3 ♗c5 18 ♖ac1 ♖ac8

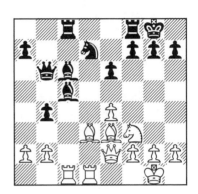

19 ♘e5?

This move is refuted by Black's fine queen 'sacrifice'. According to Semkov, White can keep a small edge with 19 ♗a6!, for example 19...♗xe3 20 ♗xc8 ♗xc1 21 ♗xd7 ♗f4 22 ♗xc6 ♕xc6 23 e5 g6 24 g3 ♗h6 25 ♖d4.

19...♗xe3 20 ♖xc6 ♗xf2+ 21 ♔f1 ♘xe5!!

Perhaps White missed this idea.

22 ♖xb6 ♗xb6 23 g3

Materially speaking the position is roughly level, but I very much prefer Black's rook, knight and pawn to White's queen. Here the queen is clearly in a passive role, having to defend White's king, and it's never happy doing this mundane task. Meanwhile there is not even a sniff of counterplay against Black's own king, which for the moment is very safe.

One further aspect of this position that becomes important in certain lines is the presence of opposite-coloured bishops. As I mentioned in *Simple Chess*, this feature often favours the player with the initiative. If he concentrates his attack on the colour of squares of his bishop, it sometimes seems as if he is playing with an extra piece.

23...h5!

In some ways this is a paradoxical decision, as White is now allowed what seems like undeserved counterplay against Black's king. However, concrete analysis shows that Black is winning if White captures on h5, so this has to be correct. Nevertheless, Black can if he wishes take a safer option (something like 23...♖c7 or 23...♖d8, or ...g7-g6 followed by ...h7-h5) which would still leave him with a clear advantage. White's weaknesses will not go away.

24 ♕xh5

Otherwise White has to contend with the threat of ...♘g4.

24...♘xd3!

Shades of Fischer-Petrosian (see Chapter 2). It's another case of a 'bad' bishop being a good defender (here it is the c2-square), so Black is quite happy to exchange it even though it means giving up a well-placed knight.

25 ♖xd3 ♖c2

Now we see the point of 23...h5!. The rook hits the seventh rank and before long the other rook on f8 joins its partner.

26 ♔e1 g6 27 ♕h6 ♖fc8 28 g4

White goes for a desperate counter-attack with queen and rook. This is certainly the best practical chance: the white king's position is beyond repair and the queen and rook are very unhappy defenders. One example of a failed defensive try is 28 ♖d2?, which loses immediately to 28...b3! 29 axb3 ♗a5.

28...♖g2!

Making way for the other rook.

29 ♖h3

Now White threatens mate, but Semkov has it covered.

29...♗d4 30 ♕h7+ ♔f8 31 ♕h6+ ♔g8 32 ♕h7+ ♔f8 33 ♕h6+ ♔e8!

Black gets back on track.

34 ♕f4

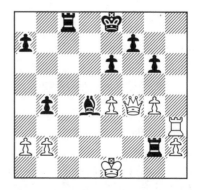

34...♖cc2?

A shame. Black could have crowned his strategy with the winning line 34...♗e5! (using the weakness of the back rank) 35 ♕e3 ♖c1+! 36 ♕xc1 ♖g1+ 37 ♔d2 ♗f4+.

35 ♔d1?

White could have put up more resistance with 35 ♖f3 f6 36 ♕b8+ ♔f7 37 ♕b7+ ♔g8 38 ♕b8+ ♔g7 39 ♕b7+ ♔h6 40 g5+! ♔xg5 41 ♖g3+ (Semkov), forcing the exchange of rooks. After 41...♖xg3 42 hxg3 ♖xb2 Black still has some work to do.

35...♖xb2

Now Black is winning again. The forthcoming queen checks are less dangerous than they look.

36 ♕b8+ ♔d7 37 ♕b7+ ♔d8 38 ♕b8+ ♔d7 39 ♕b7+ ♔d6!

40 e5+

Or 40 ♕b8+ ♔c6 41 ♕e8+ ♔c5 42 ♕c8+ ♔b5 43 ♕d7+ ♔a5 44 ♕d8+ ♗b6 45 ♕g5+ ♔a4 and Black finally escapes the checks, leaving White defenceless on the back rank. That said, I doubt if Semkov envisaged so much apparent counterplay for White when playing 23...h5 !

40...♔xe5 41 ♕c7+ ♔d5 42 ♕d7+

♔c4 43 ♕c6+ ♗c5 44 ♕e4+ ♔b5 45 ♔c1 ♖xa2 0-1

White has a few more 'spite checks' (46 ♕b7+ ♔a5 47 ♕c7+ ♗b6 48 ♕e5+ ♔a4), after which 49 ♔b1 ♖ae2 forces White to give up the queen.

Calvo Minguez-Kurajica
Osijek 1978
Queen's Indian Defence

1 ♘f3 ♘f6 2 c4 e6 3 ♘c3 b6 4 g3 ♗b7 5 ♗g2 ♗e7 6 0-0 0-0 7 b3 d5 8 e3 c5 9 ♗b2 ♘a6 10 ♕e2 ♘e4 11 cxd5 exd5 12 d3 ♘xc3 13 ♗xc3 ♘c7 14 ♕b2 d4 15 exd4 ♘b5 16 dxc5 ♘xc3 17 ♕xc3 ♗f6 18 d4 ♖c8 19 b4 bxc5 20 bxc5 ♗xf3 21 ♕xf3 ♗xd4 22 ♖ad1 ♖xc5 23 ♖d3 ♕f6

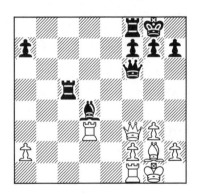

24 ♖fd1!

A profound idea, tempting Black to 'win' a queen for rook and bishop.

24...♖f5

Black goes for it. The 'safer' way out was with 24...♕xf3 25 ♗xf3 ♗f6 but after 26 ♖d7! followed by ♗d5 Black will still have to work hard for the draw.

25 ♕xf5 ♕xf5 26 ♖xd4

At first sight it's difficult to believe that White has any advantage here. Black is slightly ahead on material and there doesn't seem to be much going on in the position (both kings look quite safe). However, White has a very specific plan in mind: to attack the pawn on f7. As mentioned before, the queen and rook are not happy defenders and this is partly because they are so highly valued. White intends to pile up on f7 and use his 'extra' piece to the full effect.

26...g6 27 ♗d5!

White's plan is safe and very easy to carry out. Black has little in the way of counterplay.

27...♔g7 28 ♗b3 h5

Black doesn't have time to activate his rook; for example, 28...♖e8? is met by 29 ♖f4!, when f7 drops immediately.

29 h4 a6 30 ♖d7 ♔h6

If Black remains passive then White simply uses his numerical superiority: 30...♕f6 31 ♖a7 ♕b6 32 ♖dd7 ♕f6 and now the simple 33 ♖xf7+! shows one reason why the queen is such a bad defender – it obviously doesn't like being 'exchanged'! Following 33...♖xf7 34 ♖xf7+ ♕xf7 35 ♗xf7 ♔xf7 36 ♔g2 White has a winning king and pawn ending.

31 ♖a7 ♕f6 32 ♖dd7

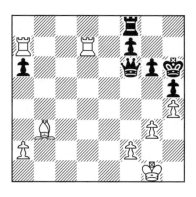

32...g5?

I can understand Black's wish to create counterplay, but this move only further weakens his king, a dangerous idea when White still retains both rooks. Black would do better just to give up on the f7-pawn with something like 32...♕b6 33 ♖xf7 ♖xf7 34 ♖xf7 ♕d6, after which White's winning chances are quite slim due to the lack of material.

33 hxg5+ ♕xg5 34 ♗xf7 ♕f6 35 ♖e7! ♔g5

Or 35...♕a1+ 36 ♔g2 ♔g5 (36...♖xf7 37 ♖xf7 ♕xa2 38 ♖f6+ ♔g5 39 ♖axa6 is an easy win for White) 37 ♖xa6 ♔f5 38 ♗g6+ ♔g4 39 ♗d3 and Black's king is in a mating net; for example, 39...h4 40 ♖g6+ ♔h5 41 g4 mate.

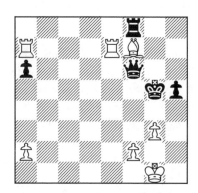

36 ♖e6?

White misses an easy win with 36 ♖e5+! ♚g4 (or 36...♕xe5 37 f4+) 37 ♗e6+ ♚f3 38 ♖e3 mate.

36...♕d4

36...♖xf7 37 ♖xf6 ♖xf6 38 ♖a8! (Marjanovic; 38 ♚g2? h4! is less clear) doesn't hold out much hope for Black, as the attempt to simplify with 38...h4 is met by 39 ♖g8+!.

37 ♖exa6 h4?

A blunder in an admittedly very difficult position. Black's only way to defend was with 37...♖c8! (threatening to obtain counterplay with ...♖c1+) 38 ♖g6+ ♚f5 39 ♖a5+ ♖c5, and now 40 ♖xc5+ ♕xc5 41 ♖h6?? loses a rook to 41...♕c1+, while 40 ♖ga6 h4! gives Black some drawing chances.

38 ♖g6+ ♚f5 39 ♖a5+ 1-0

39...♚e4 40 ♖g4+ wins the queen.

After eating the poisoned pawn: fighting or running away?

One strength that separates the greats from the rest of the crowd is the ability to use the queen effectively in difficult situations. Here I would like to look at the case of the queen being on its own deep in enemy territory, typically after having grabbed a 'poisoned pawn'. I've noticed that in many examples the player's instinct tells him, with the goods intact, to retreat the queen back to 'safety' as soon as possible. A thoroughly understandable decision, but often this isn't the best solution. I know we should always assess each position on its own merits, and that it's always dangerous to come up with sweeping generalisations (and it's also severely embarrassing to have your queen trapped!), but I would

say that more often than not it seems better for the queen to hang around its crime scene, so to speak. One justification for this is that by grabbing a pawn, the queen has created a serious weakness in the opponent's camp that may be exploited. By staying and 'fighting its corner', the queen actually provides excellent nuisance value and in many cases slows down the gambiteer's initiative.

Let's begin by looking at probably the most famous pawn-grab: the Poisoned Pawn variation of the Najdorf Sicilian. Of course here Black has reams of theory to fall back on, so there is less need for independent thought. But let's see if the theory agrees with the principle of the queen fighting its corner.

1 e4 c5 2 ♘f3 d6 3 d4 cxd4 4 ♘xd4 ♘f6 5 ♘c3 a6 6 ♗g5 e6 7 f4 ♕b6 8 ♕d2 ♕xb2 9 ♖b1 ♕a3

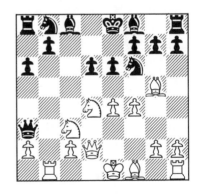

10 f5 ♘c6

Instead of this important developing move, this is Black's first chance to retreat his queen to 'safety', but is it worth it? Let's check out the lines:

a) Unsurprisingly 10...♕c5? runs into immediate trouble after 11 fxe6 fxe6 12 ♗xf6 gxf6 13 ♘a4! (the problem with

...♕c5; that b6-square is looking inviting!) 13...♗h6 (13...♕c7 14 ♘b6 ♖a7 15 ♗c4 is simply woeful for Black) 14 ♕xh6 ♕xd4 (or 14...♕a5+ 15 c3 ♕xa4 16 ♗e2! ♕a5 17 ♗h5+ ♔d8 18 ♕xf6+ and Black resigned, Willberg-Pahta, correspondence 1967) 15 ♘b6 ♖a7 16 ♕g7! ♕c3+ 17 ♔d1 ♖f8 18 ♗e2! ♕d4+ 19 ♔e1 ♕c3+ 20 ♔f1 and there is no good way to deal with the decisive threat of ♗h5+.

b) 10...♕a5?! is not quite so bad, but Black is way behind in development and faces a very strong attack: 11 fxe6 fxe6 12 ♗c4 (again it's the weakness at e6 that White pinpoints) 12...d5 13 e5!

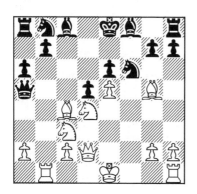

and now Black has a difficult choice:

b1) 13...dxc4 14 0-0! and Black is highly unlikely to survive the onslaught, for example:

b11) 14...♘g4 15 ♕f4 ♘xe5 16 ♖be1 ♘bd7 17 ♕f7+!! ♘xf7 18 ♖xe6+ ♗e7 19 ♖xe7+ ♔f8 20 ♘e6+ ♔g8 21 ♖e8+ (Nunn) and it's mate next move.

b12) 14...♘d5 15 ♕f2! ♕c7 16 ♘e4 (intending ♘d6+) 16...♘c6 17 ♘d6+ ♗xd6 18 exd6 ♕d7 19 ♘xe6! ♕xe6 20 ♖be1 and White is winning.

b2) 13...♗b4 14 ♖xb4! ♕xb4 15 ♗e2 ♘g8 16 0-0 (threatening ♕f4 or ♗h5+

followed by ♕f2) 16...♘c6? (a mistake, but it's unlikely Black can survive even with stronger defence) 17 ♘xc6 bxc6 18 ♘b5!! c5 (18...♕xd2 allows a nice mate after 19 ♘d6+ ♔d7 20 ♖f7+ ♘e7 21 ♖xe7+ ♔d8 22 ♘f7) 19 ♕xb4 cxb4 20 ♘c7+ ♔d7 21 ♘xa8 and White won easily in Maeder-Kondratiev, correspondence 1974.

11 fxe6

Now comes a passage where Black has little choice with his moves.

11...fxe6 12 ♘xc6 bxc6 13 e5 dxe5

The other option is 13...♘d5.

14 ♗xf6 gxf6 15 ♘e4

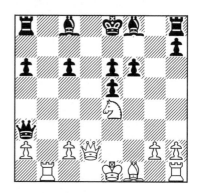

Now the main line runs 15...♗e7 16 ♗e2 h5 17 ♖b3 ♕a4, after which White chooses between the immediate 18 c4 (preventing Black's queen from coming to d4), to which Black plays 18...f5!, and the sacrifice 18 ♘xf6+ ♗xf6 19 c4. There's an incredible amount of theory on this line and the overall assessment is that Black is okay.

Going back to the position after 15 ♘e4, there's a temptation for Black to rush his queen back into defence but the variations show that this is not a good idea.

15...♕e7?! 16 ♗e2 h5

Black must prevent ♗h5+.

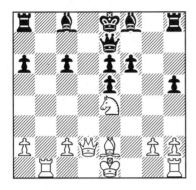

17 ♕d1!

After a few other tries, White eventually came to this move, which forces the bishop to h5. Note that the white queen has more freedom of movement now that Black's queen is no longer hanging around the weakened queenside.

17...♗g7 18 ♗xh5+ ♔f8 19 0-0 f5 20 ♖b3 ♔g8 21 ♖d3

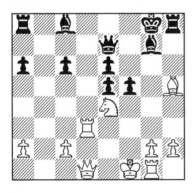

21...a5

Giving the bishop an escape square on a6. 21...fxe4 loses to 22 ♗f7+! ♕xf7 23 ♖d8+ so the only other alternative is 21...♖a7 22 ♖d8+ ♔h7 (Ralbjerg-Nagel, correspondence 1991) 23 ♗e8!! and White is winning, for example:

a) 23...♗h6 24 ♖xc8 ♖xe8 25 ♖xe8

♕xe8 26 ♘f6+.

b) 23...♖f8 24 ♕h5+ ♔g8 25 ♘g5 ♗h6 26 ♗f7+.

c) 23...♕h4 24 g3! ♕h6 25 ♖xc8 fxe4 26 ♕e2 (Nagel).

22 ♖d8+! ♔h7 23 ♗f7 ♕h4 24 ♖d3 ♗h6 25 ♖h3!

Much stronger than 25 ♘d6 ♖f8 26 ♕e2 ♗a6 27 ♕xe5 ♗xd3 28 cxd3 ♖ad8 29 ♗xe6 ♗g7 30 ♗xf5+ ♔h8, when Black was better in Van Houten-Nagel, correspondence 1988.

25...♕xe4 26 ♕h5 ♔g7 27 ♕g6+ ♔f8 28 ♗xe6!

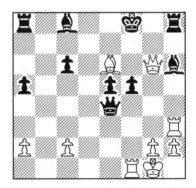

28...♗xe6

Or:

a) 28...♔e7 29 ♕f7+ ♔d6 30 ♖d1+ ♔c5 31 ♕e7+.

b) 28...♕d4+ 29 ♔h1 ♔e7 30 ♕f7+ ♔d6 31 ♗xc8 ♖axc8 32 ♖d3 and White won in Marcotulli-Jones, correspondence 2000.

29 ♕f6+ ♔e8 30 ♕xe6+

and Black resigned in the game Boto-Mijatovic, Yugoslavia 1991 due to 30 ♕xe6+ ♔d8 31 ♖d1+ ♔c7 32 ♕e7+ ♔b8 33 ♖b1+.

I suppose it's true that someone could come along and patch up this line for Black, but it just feels too risky for Black to survive. Instead the queen does a good job on a3. Such a good job that White's best line is to actually sacrifice a knight to keep the black queen temporarily out of the game (see the note to White's 15th move).

In the following snippet it's the renowned grandmaster Ljubomir Ljubojevic who makes the mistake of opting for 'safety first'.

Timman-Ljubojevic
Hilversum (5th matchgame) 1987
Queen's Gambit Declined

1 d4 ♘f6 2 c4 e6 3 ♘c3 d5 4 cxd5 exd5 5 ♗g5 c6 6 e3 ♘bd7 7 ♗d3 ♗d6 8 ♘f3 ♘f8 9 ♘e5 ♕b6 10 0-0 ♕xb2 11 ♖c1 ♘g6 12 f4 0-0 13 ♖c2

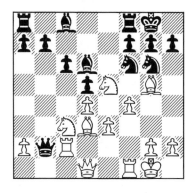

13...♕b6?
Ljubojevic's instinct is to retreat as far as possible, but on this occasion the queen should have 'stayed in the mixer' with 13...♕a3!. The point is that if White reacts as in the game with 14 ♗xf6 gxf6 15 ♘g4 ♗xg4 16 ♕xg4 Black has the important resource 16...♗b4!, which very much justifies the queen going to the a3-square.

14 ♗xf6 gxf6 15 ♘g4 ♗xg4

This is forced, as 15...♗g7 16 f5 ♘e7 17 ♘xf6! ♔xf6 18 ♕h5 (Timman) gives White a winning attack. However, now White wins a crucial pawn.

16 ♕xg4 ♔h8 17 ♖b1 ♕c7 18 ♘xd5 ♕d8 19 ♘c3 ♗xf4 20 ♖e2!

Now White has an undisputed advantage, as bishop retreats will simply be met by 21 ♖xb7. Instead Ljubojevic played 20...♖e8 21 ♘e4 ♗xe3+?! 22 ♖xe3 ♕xd4 but after 23 ♖be1 Timman went on to win.

The following game, featuring a sharp line in the Modern Benoni that I have played as Black from time to time, once again provides a situation where the queen has to decide whether to fight or run away. On this occasion it's the white queen that grabs the b-pawn.

Crouch-Povah
Portsmouth 2003
Modern Benoni

1 d4 ♘f6 2 c4 e6 3 ♘f3 c5 4 d5 exd5 5 cxd5 d6 6 ♘c3 g6 7 e4 a6 8 a4 ♗g4 9 ♕b3!?

In some ways this is a critical test of

8...♗g4, but it certainly isn't risk-free for White! 9 ♗e2 is the standard move.

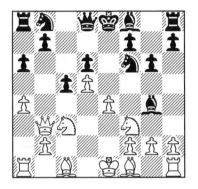

9...♗xf3

The only consistent response. Protecting b7 with 9...♕c7 allows White to move his f3-knight. Following 10 ♘d2! the bishop is looking rather silly on g4.

10 ♕xb7

Again the critical move. Recapturing on f3 allows Black time to protect b7 with ...♕c7.

10...♘bd7!?

The sharpest – Black has no qualms about sacrificing a pawn. However, 10...♗xg2!? 11 ♔xg2 ♘bd7, keeping the material balance, is also playable.

11 gxf3 ♗g7

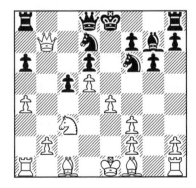

12 ♕b3?

White chooses 'safety first', but the upshot of this is that Black is now free to pursue his initiative without any distractions – a very pleasant practical situation to have.

Probably the strongest continuation is the brave 12 ♕c6!, when White continues to play ambitiously by attacking d6. The flipside to this approach is that there is always the danger that the queen will wind up getting trapped, but if you worry about this then you probably shouldn't be grabbing pawns with your queen in the opening!

Let's briefly examine a couple of possible lines:

a) 12...♕b8 13 a5! is assessed as better for White by Benoni expert Lev Psakhis. The weakness on a6 is fixed and White's queen has a handy retreat square on a4 (when the time is right).

b) Probably Black must be bold and offer the d-pawn too: 12...0-0! 13 ♕xd6 ♘h5 14 f4! (the enticing 14 ♗h3 can be met effectively by 14...f5! – threatening to trap the queen with ...♖f6 – 15 ♕e6+ ♔h8 16 d6 ♘e5 17 ♔e2 ♕h4 18 ♗g2 ♘d3! 19 ♔xd3 ♕xf2 when Black's position looks very promising) 14...♖e8 15 ♗e2! ♖a7 (again Black prepares to trap the queen, but I think that White should ignore this!) 16 ♗xh5! ♗f8 (16...gxh5? 17 ♖g1 ♔h8 18 a5 ♕h4 19 ♗e3 ♖c8 20 ♖xg7! ♔xg7 21 0-0-0 looks grim for Black) 17 ♕c6 ♘b8 18 ♕xe8 ♕xe8 19 ♗f3 and White has a rook, bishop, pawn and a strong centre for the queen. Perhaps he is a little bit better.

Again it's true that someone could come along and improve on Black's play in these lines, and the assessment of 12 ♕c6 is probably just 'unclear'. On the other hand I can confidently state that Black is better after 12 ♕b3?. Not only this, his position is also very easy to play – a very important practical consideration.

12...0-0 13 ♕d1

One of the earliest games in this line happened to be one of my own. Kurz-Emms, Baden Baden 1992 continued 13 ♗e2 ♘h5! 14 h4 ♗e5 15 ♗g5 ♕a5 16 ♗d2 ♗f4 17 ♕c2 ♕d8 18 ♘d1 ♘e5 19 ♘e3 ♕f6 and Black has an enormous grip on the dark squares. The game concluded 20 ♖h3 ♗h6 21 ♘g4 ♗xd2+ 22 ♕xd2 ♕g7 23 ♘e3 ♖fb8 24 ♘d1 ♖b3 25 ♖c1 ♕f6 26 ♖c3 ♖xc3 27 ♕xc3 ♘f4 28 ♖h2 c4 29 ♔d2 ♘xe2 30 ♔xe2 ♖b8 31 ♖h3 ♖b3 32 ♕c1 ♘xf3 33 ♖g3 ♘d4+ 34 ♔e1 ♕xh4 35 ♕xc4 ♕xe4+ 36 ♔f1 ♖xg3 37 fxg3 ♕h1+ and White resigned.

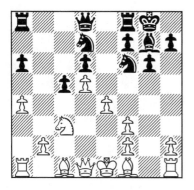

13...♘h5!

Following the same route as the game in the previous note. Black utilises White's dodgy pawn structure on the kingside to fight for control of the dark squares.

14 f4

The logical way to fight back, but it seems that White is fighting a losing bat-

tle. He has simply fallen too far behind in development by continuously moving the queen.

14...♕h4 15 ♕f3 f5!

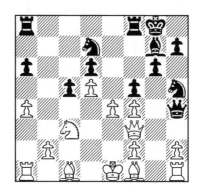

Of course! Black opens up the position with White's king stuck in the centre. The results are disastrous for White.

16 exf5 ♖xf5 17 ♕h3 ♖e8+ 18 ♗e3 ♗xc3+!

Black can even afford to part with his beloved Benoni bishop!

19 bxc3 ♕f6 20 ♔d2

Or 20 ♖c1 ♘xf4 21 ♕g3 ♖g5 22 ♕h4 ♖e4 and it's a complete massacre.

20...♘xf4 21 ♗xf4 ♖xf4 22 ♗xa6 ♖xf2+ 23 ♔d1 ♕f4 0-1

White must give up his queen or get mated, for example 24 ♕d3 ♖e3 25 ♕b1 ♖e1+ 26 ♔xe1 ♕d2 mate.

Replacing the bishop

When one of the bishop pair has been exchanged, the queen often finds itself well placed when operating on the same colour as the exchanged bishop, thus effectively taking over the bishop's role. In this way it nicely complements the remaining bishop and can also both cover defects in its own camp and exploit weaknesses in the enemy position on this colour.

I'm sure I'd already used this principle before playing this game, but I remember being pleased with the straightforward way that my queen replaced the dark-squared bishop here. It seemingly led to an easy win without much effort.

Emms-Kraschl
Cappelle la Grande 1993
Sicilian Defence

1 e4 c5 2 ♘f3 e6 3 d4 cxd4 4 ♘xd4 ♘f6 5 ♘c3 d6 6 f4 a6 7 ♕f3 ♕b6 8 ♘b3 ♕c7 9 g4 b5 10 ♗d3 ♗b7 11 g5 ♘fd7 12 ♗e3 ♘c5 13 0-0-0 ♘c6 14 ♔b1 g6 15 h4 b4 16 ♘e2 ♘a4 17 h5 ♗g7 18 ♘ed4 ♘xd4 19 ♗xd4 ♗xd4 20 ♘xd4 0-0-0 21 ♘b3 ♘c5

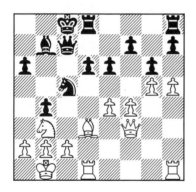

22 ♕e3!

It just seems so natural for the queen to play on the dark squares.

22...♔b8 23 ♕d4!

Eyeing both the pawn on b4 and the dark-squared weaknesses on the kingside.

23...♘xb3 24 axb3 ♕c5 25 ♕g7! ♕c7 26 ♖h4

Threatening simply to double on the h-file. White already has a decisive ad-

vantage without having to play any special moves.

The game concluded 26...gxh5 27 ♖xh5 ♕e7 28 ♖xh7 ♖xh7 29 ♕xh7 e5 30 f5 ♕xg5 31 ♕xf7 d5 32 exd5 ♗xd5 33 ♕g6 ♕xg6 34 fxg6 ♗e4 35 g7 ♗xd3 36 ♖xd3 ♖g8 37 ♖d7 e4 38 ♖f7 and my opponent resigned.

By the time I played the following game, I was more on the lookout for this particular idea.

Emms-Dautov
Germany 1994
Ruy Lopez

1 e4 e5 2 ♘f3 ♘c6 3 ♗b5 g6 4 c3 a6 5 ♗a4 d6 6 d4 ♗d7 7 0-0 ♗g7 8 ♖e1 ♘ge7 9 ♗e3 0-0 10 ♘bd2 h6 11 dxe5 dxe5 12 ♗b3 ♕c8 13 a4 b6 14 ♗a2 a5 15 ♘c4 ♗e6

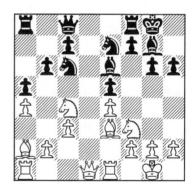

16 ♕b1!

I remember feeling very pleased with this move. The plan is to play ♘a3-b5, inducing Black to exchange on a2. After the trade of light-squared bishops the white queen will sit very comfortably on the important a2-g8 diagonal.

16...♔h7 17 ♘a3 f5 18 ♘b5 ♗xa2

19 ♕xa2 f4 20 ♗d2 g5 21 h3 ♗f6 22 ♘h2 h5 23 f3

Black has gained some space on the kingside and White has a poorly placed knight on h2. Nevertheless, White still holds an edge, due to his light-squared control. In particular, Black must lose time eliminating the knight from b5.

23...♘a7 24 ♘xa7 ♖xa7 25 ♖ed1 ♘g8 26 ♗e1 ♘h6 27 ♕c4 g4 28 hxg4 hxg4 29 fxg4 ♘xg4 30 ♕c6!

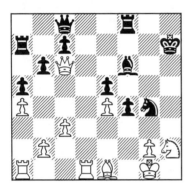

White's queen continues to dominate the light squares. Now Black cannot allow White to infiltrate with ♖d7.

30...♖f7 31 ♖d3 ♘xh2 32 ♔xh2 ♖a8 33 ♖ad1 ♕e8 34 ♖d7 ♖d8!

The only defence, but a good one. White has to work hard to keep an advantage.

35 ♖xf7+ ♕xf7 36 ♖xd8 ♗xd8 37 ♔g1 ♗e7 38 ♗f2 ♗f8 39 c4?

This move should have let the advantage slip away. 39 ♔f1! is the right way. Now Black misses his chance of 39...♗b4 40 ♔f1 ♕e7!, intending to trade his 'bad' bishop with ...♗c5.

39...♕g7? 40 ♕e6?! ♗b4?!

On the final move before the first time control, once more both players err. White should have played 40 ♔f1!, while

Black misses his last chance for 40...♗c5!.

41 ♕f5+ ♔g8 42 ♕e6+ ♔h7 43 ♔f1!

Now Black really suffers on the light squares.

43...♗c5 44 ♗h4 ♗d6 45 ♔f2 ♕g6 46 ♕d7+ ♔g8 47 ♔f3 ♕f7 48 ♕g4+ ♔f8 49 ♕f5! ♔g8

49...♕xf5 50 exf5 wins, as White has obtained the vital e4-square for the king.

50 b3

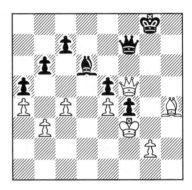

Black is in a virtual zugzwang. 50...♔f8 51 ♕g4 is terminal, while 50...♗e7 51 ♕xf7+ ♔xf7 52 ♗xe7 ♔xe7 53 ♔g4 ♔f6 54 ♔h5! leads to a winning king and pawn endgame.

50...♕e8 51 ♗f6 c6

51...♕f7 52 ♔g4 wins in a similar fashion.

52 ♕g5+ ♔f7 53 ♕h5+ ♔f8 54 ♕xe8+ ♔xe8 55 ♔g4 1-0

White's mastery of the light squares continue to the end – the white king enters f5 with decisive effect.

Finding a suitable home

Often one of the most important decisions in an opening or early middlegame is where to place the queen. Just talking about the white queen for the moment, regular jumping points include a4, b3, c2, e2, f3, g4, h5, d2 and d3, while on occasions it's simply best left at home on d1. Strong players are particularly adept at finding the right square for the queen to rest, even if this square isn't the first that comes to mind. Below I've selected a couple of examples of this.

Kramnik-Timman
Belgrade 1995
Queen's Gambit Declined

1 ♘f3 ♘f6 2 c4 e6 3 ♘c3 d5 4 d4 ♘bd7 5 cxd5 exd5 6 ♗g5 c6 7 e3 ♗e7 8 ♗d3 ♘h5 9 ♗xe7 ♕xe7 10 0-0 0-0

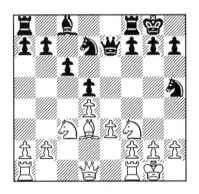

White could continue in 'normal' fashion with 11 ♕c2, hitting the h7-pawn or 11 ♖b1, preparing a typical minority attack on the queenside, but Kramnik uses his imagination just a little and sees a way of doing two things at once.

11 ♕b1! ♘hf6 12 b4
and White has a clear edge.

Black's non-stereotyped way of activating his queen in this second example very much appealed to me.

Kavalek-Liberzon
Amsterdam 1977
Sicilian Defence

1 e4 c5 2 ♘f3 e6 3 d4 cxd4 4 ♘xd4 ♘c6 5 ♘b5 d6 6 c4 ♘f6 7 ♘5c3 ♗e7 8 ♗e2 0-0 9 0-0 b6 10 ♗f4 ♗b7 11 ♖e1 ♖c8 12 ♗f1 ♘e5 13 ♘d2 ♘fd7 14 ♗g3

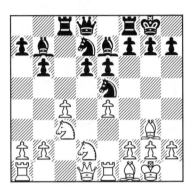

14...g5!
This is a sharp way of counterattacking in hedgehog positions. Black plans ...♔h8 and ...♖g8 etc.

15 ♖c1 a6 16 f3
I'm not sure if I like this move. It gives the e-pawn extra support, but now Black has a 'hook' for a later ...g5-g4.

16...♔h8 17 ♗f2 ♖g8

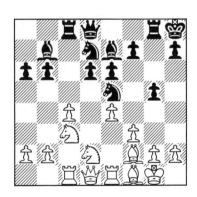

18 h3?!

This gives Black more to bite onto on the kingside. 18 b4 was preferable.

18...♖g7! 19 b4 h5! 20 a3

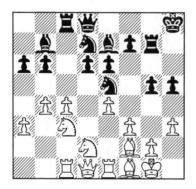

20...♕g8!! 21 ♖e3 ♕h7

Not exactly a hackneyed approach by Black! In fact I'm not sure if I've seen this manoeuvre in this type of position before, but here it is mightily effective. Black intends to follow up with ...♖cg8, after which his major pieces unconditionally support further kingside action.

22 ♘e2 ♖cg8 23 ♖cc3 ♖g6 24 f4

This weakens White further, but Black was going to break with ...g5-g4 anyway.

24...gxf4 25 ♘xf4 ♖h6 26 ♖g3 ♖xg3 27 ♗xg3 h4 28 ♗f2 ♗xe4

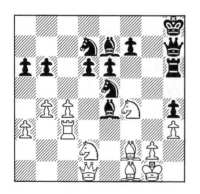

Black has won a crucial pawn and

White's position collapses.

29 c5 dxc5 30 bxc5 ♗xc5 31 ♗xc5 bxc5 32 ♘c4 ♕f5! 33 ♕d2 ♖f6 34 ♘xe5 ♘xe5 35 ♕d8+ ♔g7 36 g3 ♘f3+ 37 ♖xf3 ♗xf3 38 ♗d3 ♕e5 0-1

Of course one must always be wary of moving the queen to the edge or where it may interfere with the ability of some of the other pieces, especially if the position suddenly opens up. The following example is included to redress the balance to a certain extent and show the dangers of an absent queen.

De Vreugt-Hector
Wijk aan Zee 2003
Ruy Lopez

1 e4 e5 2 ♘f3 ♘c6 3 ♗b5 a6 4 ♗a4 ♘f6 5 0-0 b5 6 ♗b3 ♗b7 7 ♖e1 ♗c5 8 c3 d6 9 d4 ♗b6 10 ♗e3 0-0 11 ♘bd2 h6 12 h3 ♖e8

A typical move in the Ruy Lopez. Black indirectly hits the e-pawn and now threatens ...exd4.

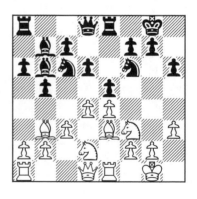

13 ♕b1!?

Both ♕c2 and ♗c2 allow Black ideas with ...exd4, cxd4, ...♘b4!, hence the finesse of the text. I actually advocated this move in my book *Easy Guide to the Ruy Lopez*, but after seeing Black's impressive display here, I'm beginning to have second thoughts. Perhaps White should make do with closing the centre with 13 d5.

13...♘b8!

Hector plays as in the Breyer Defence. This knight retreat adds further pressure to e4, so White must again react. Black's plan in to re-route the knight to the excellent d7-square and then hit White in the centre with either ...c5 or ...d5, and this idea seems to promise equality.

In contrast, 13...♘a5 14 ♗c2 c5 15 d5 c4 16 b4 cxb3 17 axb3 ♗c8 18 b4 ♘b7 19 c4 was slightly better for White in Rowson-Emms, British League 1997.

14 ♗c2 ♘bd7 15 b4

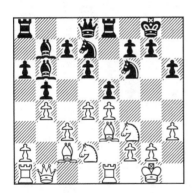

15...d5!

An excellent move. Now in many lines the centre is blasted completely open, and White has to be careful that his queen on b1 doesn't get left out of the action.

16 dxe5 dxe4!?

An ambitious idea. GM Tom Wedberg, annotating this game for *ChessBase Magazine*, gives an alternative and safer

route for Black with 16...♗xe3 17 ♖xe3 ♘xe5 18 ♘xe5 dxe4! when Black regains his piece with at least equality (18...♖xe5 19 ♘f3 ♖e8 20 e5 may be a touch better for White).

17 ♘xe4

White can win a pawn with 17 exf6 exf3 18 ♗h7+ ♔h8 19 fxg7+ ♔xg7 20 ♘xf3 but after 20...♗xf3 21 gxf3 ♗xe3 22 fxe3 ♕h4! 23 ♖e2 ♘f6 24 ♗f5 ♔h8 Black has a menacing attack on the kingside.

17...♘xe5

Black already has some advantage. The position has opened up, with Black having the more active pieces and White's queen beginning to look a little silly on b1!

18 ♘xe5 ♖xe5

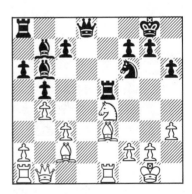

19 ♖d1

There's no easy solution to White's problems, for example:

a) 19 ♗f4? ♖xe4! 20 ♗xe4 ♘xe4 21 ♖xe4 ♕d5! and Black wins.

b) 19 ♗xb6 cxb6 20 ♘xf6+ ♕xf6 21 ♖xe5 ♕xe5 22 ♕e1 ♕g5 and White is forced to grovel with 23 ♕f1.

19...♕e7 20 ♗c5 ♗xc5 21 ♘xc5 ♗c6 22 ♕c1?

Understandably White is eager to get

his queen back into play, but it was already necessary to deal with the concrete threats. 22 ♗d3 (Wedberg), preparing the defensive ♗f1, was mandatory.

22...♖g5!

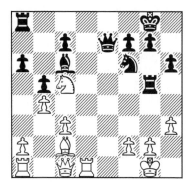

Now Black's straightforward attack on the white king is simply winning.

23 g3 ♕e2!

Threatening the decisive ...♖xg3+!.

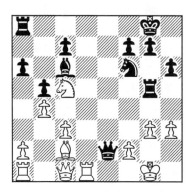

24 ♖d3 ♖xc5! 25 bxc5 ♘e4 0-1

Exercises

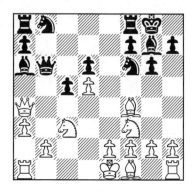

Exercise 4.1 White to play

Black has just played the move ...♕d8-b6, attacking White's b2-pawn. White has two sensible-looking ways of dealing with this threat: ♕c2 and ♖b1. Which do you prefer?

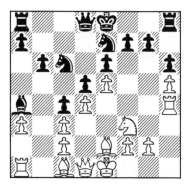

Exercise 4.2 Black to play

Can you spot a good 'home' for the black queen?

CHAPTER FIVE

Concerning Kings

Knowing how to use your king effectively is perhaps one of the most difficult skills in chess. Beginners often underestimate the importance of king safety and are quite happy leaving their king in the centre and opening up various lines in front of it. More experienced players, while realising the dangers of exposure in the opening and middlegame, are sometimes guilty of under-using their king in endgames, leaving it behind a solid wall of pawns away from the rest of the action when in fact there is little danger and its presence could be very useful.

In this chapter I'd like to take a look at one or two different aspects of king use, including the age-old castling question, using the king as an active piece and finally a rather light-hearted look at some 'king calamities' in the endgame.

Castling by condition?

Only castle when one can't see anything better. – Edmar Mednis in *How to Beat Bobby Fischer*

While researching for this book I came across a rather delightful article on the Internet called *Winning without Castling* (at the address www.scottishcca.co.uk), by the Latvian correspondence player Nickolai Gurtovoi. He is very much in favour of king activity and quotes Steinitz's words: 'I play the king all over the board! I make him battle! With his help, I have a superfluous piece. What about Morphy? He castles; he hides his king in a safe place...' (I think he meant superfluous in the good sense here.)

Gurtovoi is also clearly of the opinion that castling is an over-rated idea: '...Subsequent theoreticians over the last 200 years, to put it mildly, have bamboozled millions of chess players on the necessity of castling. Unfortunately now castling has assumed epidemic proportions, even amongst famous chess players, and for that reason they quite often lose.'

Gurtovoi goes on to give three defects of castling:

1) It is a waste of a tempo
2) The king is not involved in the play
3) Pieces are in disharmony (that is why the king is in danger)

and then presents over sixty games (many his own) in which players are either punished for castling or rewarded for avoiding castling.

While it's safe to say that I certainly don't agree with some of his views and assessments in the games (I don't understand his third defect, for example), this thought-provoking piece did get me wondering. I think it is quite true that the values of castling are drummed into young players from very early on, so much so that they do to some extent become conditioned to castling whatever the situation at the board, whether it is suitable to do so or not. Whether this conditioning is more powerful than similar programming such as 'control the centre' and 'knights on the rim are grim' is unclear, but there have certainly been some high-level cases of bad castling decisions.

One of the more obvious cases where castling is unsuitable is when it would involve running into a direct attack in full flow. Perhaps one of the most famous instances of a player 'castling into it' is this instructive miniature, in which one of the world's leading players makes the mistake.

Keres-Botvinnik

Soviet Championship 1941

Nimzo-Indian Defence

1 d4 ♘f6 2 c4 e6 3 ♘c3 ♗b4 4 ♕c2 d5 5 cxd5 exd5 6 ♗g5 h6 7 ♗h4 c5 8 0-0-0?

Incredibly ambitious and aggressive, but seriously flawed, as Botvinnik's lively refutation shows. Later Kasparov showed the way with the sensible 8 dxc5.

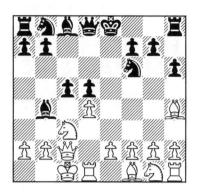

8...♗xc3!

Perhaps Keres was hoping for a repeat of the earlier game Mikenas-Botvinnik, USSR Championship, Moscow 1940, in which White claimed an advantage after 8...0-0 9 dxc5 ♗xc3 10 ♕xc3 g5 11 ♗g3 ♘e4 12 ♕a3 ♗e6 13 f3 ♘xg3 14 hxg3 ♕f6 15 e3 ♖c8 16 ♔b1 ♘d7 17 ♘e2 ♖xc5 18 ♘d4 a6 19 ♗b5! ♖ac8 20 ♗xd7 ♗xd7. However, Black doesn't have to waste time on irrelevant things like castling!

9 ♕xc3 g5! 10 ♗g3 cxd4! 11 ♕xd4 ♘c6

Black develops his queenside with a gain of time.

12 ♕a4 ♗f5!

This is obviously a good posiiton for the bishop. After the forthcoming ...♖c8 White's king will inevitably be in the firing line.

13 e3

Gurtovoi gives the alternative line 13 f3 ♕b6 14 e4 (what else can White try here?) 14...dxe4 15 ♔b1 exf3+! 16 ♔a1 ♕b4! 17 ♕xb4 ♘xb4 18 ♗b5+ ♔f8 with a winning position for Black, as 19 ♗d6+ loses after 19...♔g7 20 ♗xb4 fxg2.

13...♖c8

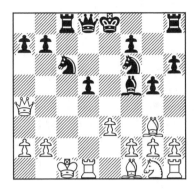

14 &d3?

After this move there's no question that White is losing. In *My Great Predecessors Volume 2,* Garry Kasparov presents quite an amusing line that's actually not that bad for White: 14 &e2 a6 15 ♕a3! b5 (or 15...&b4+ 16 &c3 ♕e7 17 &d2 &c2 18 ♖c1) 16 &d2 a5 17 ♖c1 &e4+ 18 &d1 'with an inferior but quite defensible position' – Kasparov. Here Kasparov comments that it's actually safer for White to have his king in the centre. It's quite funny how in this line White unconditionally admits his mistake on move eight, and the rook and king are busy limiting the damage created by 'uncastling'!

14...♕d7!

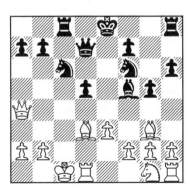

Now the major threats begin. The first is ...&b4+.

15 &b1 &xd3+ 16 ♖xd3 ♕f5!

An example of the queen effectively replacing the bishop. The rest is very straightforward for Black.

17 e4 &xe4 18 &a1 0-0

True to form, Gurtovoi suggests 18...&f8 as another possibility!

19 ♖d1

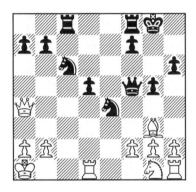

19...b5! 20 ♕xb5 &d4 21 ♕d3 &c2+! 22 &b1 &b4! 0-1

This following example is not quite so well known but leads to similar devastation.

Martin Gonzalez-Taimanov
Montilla 1977
Sicilian Defence

1 e4 c5 2 &f3 &c6 3 d4 cxd4 4 &xd4 e6 5 &c3 a6 6 &e2 &ge7 7 &e3 &xd4 8 ♕xd4 b5 9 f4 &c6 10 ♕d2 &e7 11 0-0-0?

Another case of ambition over defensive judgement. White should settle for the 'boring' 11 0-0.

11...♕a5!

I suspect that White missed the

strength of this simple move. The point is that after 12 ♗b1? (the typical reaction to a quick ...♕a5) Black has 12...b4!, when the bishop on e2 blocks the knight's 'normal' retreat and in fact there is no other good choice. After 13 ♘d5 exd5 14 exd5 Black has 14...b3! (Taimanov). White could try to defend with 12 a3 but then 12...b4! obviously gives Black a very quick attack.

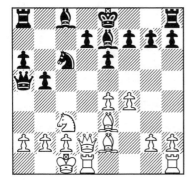

12 e5

White tries to claim compensation by moving his knight to the active d6-square.

12...b4 13 ♘e4 ♕xa2 14 ♘d6+ ♗xd6 15 ♕xd6 ♕a1+ 16 ♔d2 ♕xb2

17 ♗c5?

After 17 ♔e1! (returning the king to

the centre!) White has some play for the two pawns, but now White's king is forced back to the choppy waters of the queenside.

17...♕c3+ 18 ♔c1 b3 19 ♗d3 ♖b8 20 ♖he1 ♖b5!

Threatening both ...♖xc5 and ...♖a5.

21 ♗a3 ♘b4 22 ♖e2 b2+ 0-1

Black mates after 23 ♗xb2 ♘a2+ 24 ♔b1 ♕xb2.

In the following snippet, US grandmaster Alexander Shabalov shows some imagination to avoid the well-trodden lines of the Sicilian Dragon.

Khalifman-Shabalov
Moscow 2001
Sicilian Defence

1 e4 c5 2 ♘f3 d6 3 d4 cxd4 4 ♘xd4 ♘f6 5 ♘c3 g6 6 ♗e3 ♘c6 7 f3 ♗g7 8 ♕d2

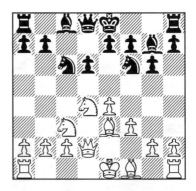

Now in over 95% of the huge number of games reaching this position on my database Black plays 8...0-0 (or 8...♗d7 followed very soon by ...0-0), but is this the only way to play? Does everyone castle here because they have been conditioned to do so?

8...h5!?

Black refuses to commit his king!

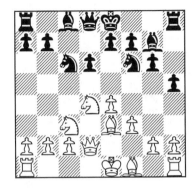

9 ♗c4 ♗d7 10 ♗b3 ♖c8

Unsurprisingly, this particular line is a great favourite of Gurtovoi's. One of his games continued 10...a6 11 0-0-0 ♘a5 12 h3 h4! (preventing g2-g4 and preparing some rook activity) 13 f4 ♖h5! (preventing 14 e5) 14 ♕f2 ♖c8! and now Black was threatening the typical Sicilian exchange sacrifice with ...♖xc3 and ...♘xe4 (Otchkov-Gurtovoi, correspondence 1993).

11 0-0-0 ♘a5 12 ♔b1 a6 13 h3 h4!

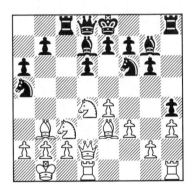

We saw this idea in the note to Black's 10th move. Again Black prevents g2-g4 and prepares ...♖h5.

14 ♖he1 ♖h5!

Give Black's rook activity, this example could easily have been placed in Chapter 6.

15 ♘de2 ♘c4 16 ♗xc4 ♖xc4 17 b3 ♖c8 18 ♘f4

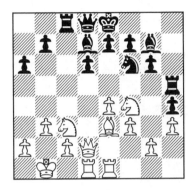

and as far as I can see, Black has a perfectly reasonable position (some might say at least as good as you would normally get from playing the Dragon; Black isn't, after all, going to be mated down the h-file!).

Here Shabalov actually erred with 18...♖e5? and following 19 ♘fd5 ♘xd5 20 ♘xd5 the threat of ♗d4 was awkward. However, in *Chess Informant* Markovic suggests the very logical move 18...♖a5. This is a very tempting move to make, especially since the natural-looking response 19 ♘cd5?? allows a spectacular win with 19...♘xd5 20 ♘xd5 ♖xa2!! 21 ♔xa2 ♖xc2+!! (take my rooks!) 22 ♕xc2 ♕a5+ 23 ♔b1 ♕a1 mate. A very nice variation which surely in itself justifies Black's way of playing!

This final example on the decision of castling is mainly included for fun, but it does demonstrate a strong grandmaster putting more important features of the position first before castling.

Sakaev-Vladimirov
Russia 2001
Nimzo-Indian Defence

1 d4 ♘f6 2 c4 e6 3 ♘c3 ♗b4 4 f3 c5 5 d5 0-0 6 e4 exd5 7 cxd5 d6 8 ♘ge2 ♘h5!? 9 g4!

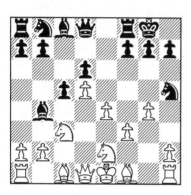

A good move. Sakaev is correct in his concern with preventing Black from gaining counterplay with ...f7-f5, even though this gives Black the option of preventing White from castling kingside.

9...♕h4+ 10 ♔d2 f5!?

Black insists on playing this move, but of course must be prepared to give up the knight.

10...♘f6 is totally inconsistent with Black's previous play. White could play a few ways against this, one possibility being 11 ♕e1 ♕xe1+ 12 ♔xe1 with a good ending.

11 gxh5 fxe4 12 ♕e1!

A novelty, and a good one (yes, this strange variation has been played before!). The earlier game Martz-Gulko, Harrachov 1967 continued 12 ♘g3 exf3 13 ♔c2 ♗xc3 14 bxc3 ♘d7 15 ♗e3 ♘e5 16 ♕d2 ♗d7 17 ♖c1 ♖ae8 and Black had reasonable compensation for the piece.

12...e3+

Black must keep the queens on the board. After 12...♕xe1+? 13 ♔xe1 exf3 14 ♘f4 (Sakaev) Black's initiative is completely killed off.

13 ♔d1

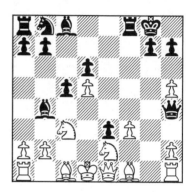

This is the real reason I included this game – the king and queen swap is very aesthetically pleasing! And the white king is actually quite safe on this square, too.

13...♕xh5 14 ♘g3! ♕xf3+ 15 ♗e2 ♕f4

Sakaev gives 15...♗xc3 as a stronger option, but White is still better after 16 ♕xc3 ♕xd5+ 17 ♔e1 (Black temporarily has four pawns for the piece but White's pieces are beginning to coordinate) 17...♗e6 18 ♖g1! ♖f7 19 ♘h5 ♕d4 20 ♗xe3 ♕xc3+ 21 bxc3, when his extra bishop is worth more than the three pawns.

16 ♖f1 ♕d4+ 17 ♔c2 ♖e8 18 ♖f3!

Threatening to round up the e3-pawn with ♕g1.

18...♕h4 19 ♖xe3 ♖xe3 20 ♗xe3 ♘d7 21 ♘ge4 ♕xh2 22 ♕f2

After 22...♕xf2 23 ♗xf2 the crucial d6-pawn drops off and Black is losing, while 22...♕e5 23 ♖f1 is not much better.

The storming king

One sign of a quality player is that he will know when and when not to use the king in an active role. The general rule given to players is that the king should be kept safe in the opening and middlegame, but is free to become active in the endgame. Of course, there are still occasions in the endgame when a king can walk into danger (we'll see a few examples later on), while conversely there have been instances of a king freely and safely advancing up the board while all the major pieces are still on. I must say that this second instance is quite rare and only occurs in special cases. There's a famous game where Nigel Short marches his king up the board to help deliver mate against Jan Timman. I won't give that here because it's been seen so many times, but the following example reminds me of it a little, as again White's king manages to shelter on the dark squares. In some ways it's even more impressive because in the Short-Timman game Black is virtually paralysed but here he is considerably more active.

Tseshkovsky-Vorotnikov
Aktjubinsk 1985

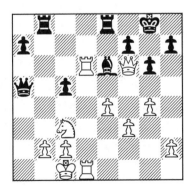

20...♕a1+ 21 ♔d2 ♕a5

Asking White the question, 'Do you have anything better than repeating the position with 23 ♔c1 here?'

21...♕xb2? loses material after 22 ♖b1 ♕a3 23 ♖xb8 ♖xb8 24 ♖xe6! fxe6 25 ♕xe6+ ♔g7 26 ♕e5+. This idea crops up on more than one occasion.

22 ♔e3!

Apparently he does!

22...c4

Now 22...♖xb2? loses to 23 ♖xe6! fxe6 24 ♖d7, but 22...c4 gives Black a defensive resource in ...♕c5+.

23 h4!

Very calm. White simply plans h4-h5-h6 and ♕g7 mate.

23...♖xb2

Now 24 ♖xe6? can be met effectively by 24...♕c5+ 25 ♔f4 fxe6 26 ♖d7 ♕f8.

24 ♔f4!

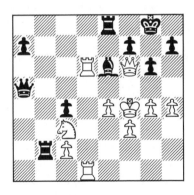

So White renews the threat! The major feature here is that White has total control of the dark squares, so his king is quite safe on this colour. In fact, if it wasn't for the black queen on a5, White would be threatening to play à la Short with ♔f4-g5-h6 and ♕g7 mate!

24...♖b6 25 ♖d8 ♖b8 26 ♖xb8 ♖xb8 27 h5 gxh5

Otherwise h5-h6 will be terminal.

28 gxh5 ♖e8

After 28...♕xh5 Tseshkovsky gives the nice line 29 ♖g1+ ♔f8 30 ♘d5! (but not 30 ♕h8+? ♔e7 31 ♕xb8? ♕h2+ 32 ♖g3 ♕d2+ 33 ♔e5 f6 and suddenly it's checkmate and White's king advance is not looking so clever after all) 30...♕h2+ 31 ♖g3 ♕d2+ 32 ♔e5!

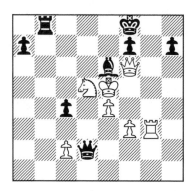

when the checks run out and Black cannot avoid mate after 32...♗xd5 33 ♕d6+ ♔e8 34 ♖g8.

29 h6 ♔f8 30 ♖g1 ♕c7+ 31 e5 1-0

Black has no good defence to the threat of ♖g8+.

The next two examples feature the much more common theme: king power in an endgame. In the first game White once again takes advantage of his control of the dark-squares (note the king uses the colour opposite to that of the opponent's bishop), while in the second case Kramnik gives a master class of how to make the most of an active king in the endgame.

Zvjaginsev-Lputian
Poikovsky 2003

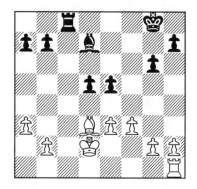

21 f4!

A good start: the white king will be very happy on the d4-square so White dislodges the pawn from e5.

21...♗c6?

A mistake. White is only a pawn up for one move as Black can easily arrange to recapture on e5. However, now White's king arrives at d4 with a tempo gain by hitting the black rook.

Zvjaginsev gives the following alternatives:

a) 21...e4? (gaining a tempo on the bishop but now Black has more pawns fixed on light squares) 22 ♗e2 h5 (or 22...♔f7 23 g4!) 23 ♖c1! ♖xc1 24 ♔xc1 ♔f7 25 ♔d2 ♔e7 26 ♔c3 ♔d6 27 ♔d4 and Zvjaginsev goes on to give some further analysis proving that White can win this endgame. This is hardly surprising given how bad Black's bishop is together with the weaknesses on g6 and d5.

b) However, both 21...♗f5 22 ♗xf5 gxf5 23 fxe5 ♔f7 24 ♖f1 ♔e6 25 ♖f3 ♔xe5 26 ♖h3 ♖c7 27 ♔d3, and 21...exf4 22 exf4 are only slightly better for White.

22 fxe5 ♖e8 23 ♔c3!

By far the strongest idea. White's king begins to show its power in this ending.

23...♖xe5 24 ♔d4 ♖g5 25 g3 ♖g4+?

After this move Black is certainly losing. The only chance was 25...♔f7.

26 ♔e5!

Of course! Did Black miss that White could answer 26...d4 with 27 e4! here?

26...♔f7 27 ♔d6!

Another excellent move, restricting the black king (preventing ...♔e7). Note that the path of White's king has consisted entirely of dark squares.

27...♔f6

The attempt to simplify with 27...d4 falls short after 28 ♖f1+ ♔g7 29 ♖f4! ♖xf4 30 exf4, after which the white king edges back to take the d4-pawn.

28 ♖f1+ ♔g5 29 ♔e5 ♖a4

30 ♖f4!

I like this move. In some ways it's quite a paradoxical idea to offer the exchange of rooks, as White's is clearly superior. However, the domination of White's king is felt even more clearly after the rooks leave the board.

30...♖xf4

Black can only avoid the exchange by putting his rook to an even more passive square. After 30...♖a5 Zvjaginsev gives 31 h4+ ♔h6 32 g4 ♔g7 33 ♔e6 ♗e8 34 ♔e7 g5 35 ♖f5 ♗g6 36 ♖xg5 as one winning line for White.

31 exf4+ ♔g4

Or 31...♔h6 32 ♗e2 followed by ♗f3.

32 f5 ♗e8

Allowing White a decisive passed pawn on f6, but 32...gxf5 33 ♗xf5+ ♔f3 34 ♗xh7 ♔e3 35 g4 d4 36 g5 d3 37 ♗xd3! ♔xd3 38 h4 is also winning.

33 f6 ♗f7 34 ♗c2 ♔h5

Or 34...d4 35 ♔xd4 ♔h3 36 ♗e4 ♔xh2 37 ♔e5 ♔xg3 38 ♗d5 ♗e8 39 ♔e6 g5 40 ♔e7 ♗h5 41 ♗f7 ♗d1 42 ♗e8 ♗b3 43 ♗d7 and ♗e6.

35 ♗b3 g5 1-0

Kramnik-Leko
Budapest (rapidplay) 2001
Grünfeld Defence

1 d4 ♘f6 2 c4 g6 3 ♘c3 d5 4 cxd5 ♘xd5 5 e4 ♘xc3 6 bxc3 ♗g7 7 ♘f3 c5 8 ♗e3 ♕a5 9 ♕d2 ♘c6 10 ♖c1 cxd4 11 cxd4 ♕xd2+ 12 ♔xd2 0-0 13 d5 ♖d8 14 ♔e1 ♘e5

14...♘a5 has been played more often, probably with good reason judging by the position Kramnik achieves.

15 ♘xe5 ♗xe5 16 f4 ♗d6 17 ♔f2 e5

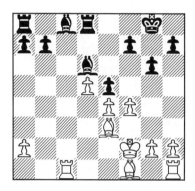

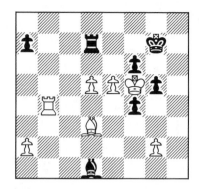

18 ♗c5!

Very logical play. This exchange offer would fit into the category of 'eliminating a defender'. Here it's Black's dark-squared bishop, which defends the key c7-square, thus preventing a rook invasion.

18...♗xc5+ 19 ♖xc5 exf4 20 ♔f3 ♗d7 21 ♗d3!

White delays capturing on f4 in order to prevent Black from claiming the c-file. Following 21 ♔xf4 ♖dc8 22 ♖xc8+ ♖xc8 23 ♗d3 ♖c3 24 ♖d1 (Kramnik) Black's active rook compensates somewhat for White's active king and central pawns.

21...♖ac8 22 ♖hc1 g5!

If White were simply allowed to recapture on f4 then Black would certainly be lost.

23 ♖c7 ♖xc7 24 ♖xc7 ♗a4

Allowing the white king to advance further, but 24...♗c8 can be met by 25 e5!.

25 ♔g4! h6 26 ♖xb7 ♖d7 27 ♖b4 ♗d1+ 28 ♔f5 ♔g7 29 h4 f6 30 hxg5 hxg5 31 e5!!

Very impressive play for a rapidplay game. This move seems to win against any defence.

31...fxe5

Kramnik shows that White is also winning after 31...♖xd5 32 ♖b7+ ♔h6 (or 32...♔h8 33 ♔g6 ♗h5+! 34 ♔xh5 ♖xd3 35 ♔g6 ♖d8 36 ♖h7+ ♔g8 37 exf6) 33 ♗b1!! ♖c5 (33...♖xe5+ 34 ♔xf6; 33...fxe5 34 ♔e6) 34 ♔xf6 ♗c2 35 ♗xc2 ♖xc2 36 e6 ♖xg2 37 ♖b8 ♔h5 38 e7 ♖e2 39 ♔f5 ♔h4 40 e8♕ ♖xe8 41 ♖xe8 f3 42 ♔e4 ♔g3 43 ♔e3 g4 44 ♖g8.

32 ♔xe5 f3 33 gxf3 ♗xf3 34 d6

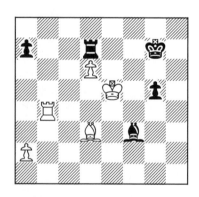

This d-pawn, supported by the far-advanced king, is a winner.

34...♖d8 35 ♗f5 ♗c6

35...♖e8+ is more resilient but still loses after 36 ♗e6 ♗c6 37 ♔f5! ♖d8 (37...♖f8+ 38 ♔xg5) 38 d7 (Kramnik).

36 d7! ♖f8 37 ♖d4 1-0

In this final example it looks like the black king is trying to help a pawn reach promotion, but in fact he has something more ambitious in mind!

Shabalov-Gelfand
Bermuda 2004

41 Rcd7+ Ke4 42 Rde7

Now after 42...e2 43 Rxe6+ Kf3 44 Rf7+ Kxg3 45 Rfe7 Black is pretty much forced to take the perpetual check on offer (45...Kf2 46 h5 isn't much help). However, Gelfand has seen that the e3-pawn is not the major player here...

42...Kf3!!

...it's the king.

43 Rxe6 Ke2!

Black's plan is revealed: ...Kd2, ...Kxc2 and ...Rb3 mate. Strangely White can do nothing useful against this idea.

44 Rd7 Kd2! 45 Rxe3

White avoids an immediate mate (45 Rxd4+ Kxc2 and ...Rb3) by giving up one of the rooks, but this only slows Black down by a couple of moves.

45...Kxe3 46 Rf7 Nd5! 47 b5 Kd2
0-1

After 48 Rf2+ Kc3 49 Rf3+ Kxc2 further resistance is useless.

King calamities

Just a little light-hearted warning before you all go off racing your kings up the board. Even in the most tranquil-looking positions there always lurks that small danger of walking your king into a mating net (in fact I'm sure it's this fear of embarrassment that prevents some players from using the full potential of the king). As the few snippets below demonstrate, even top grandmasters occasionally suffer these disasters.

Short-Beliavsky
Linares 1992

White's play in this endgame has so far been a great demonstration of how to utilise an active king. Now his domination gives him good winning chances.

57...f6+!?

A desperate measure, which surprisingly has dramatically good results for Black.

58 ♔e6??

The king marches on. Surely there's no danger?

58...♗c8 mate!

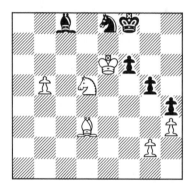

Oh dear: a very pretty self-mate! Instead of 58 ♔e6??, 58 ♘xf6 ♗xg2 59 b6 would obviously have been strong.

Barua-Spangenberg
Yerevan Olympiad 1996

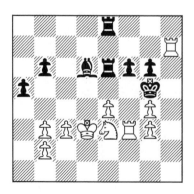

There doesn't seem to be too much danger for Black here, so the Argentinean GM grabbed the pawn with

31...♖xe4??

Only to be shocked by

32 ♖f5+!! 1-0

It's mate after 32...gxf5 33 ♖g7+! ♔h6 34 ♘xf5.

The final two examples demonstrate that the king doesn't even have to wander too far up the board to run into trouble.

Kupreichik-Ivanovic
Yugoslavia 1992

Ensuring the win for White in this position requires just a few accurate moves...

42 ♖h8 ♔xe5 43 h5?!

43 ♖a8! ♖xh4 44 a6 (Kupreichik) is clearer – Black must give up his bishop for the a6-pawn.

43...♔d5 44 h6 ♔c4

Black's king sensibly gets out of range of the white rook so that White cannot play h6-h7, rook check and then a8♕. However, there is another subtle point to Black's play...

45 h7??

...which White fails to spot. 45 ♖f8! ♖xh6 46 ♖xf4+ ♔d5 47 ♖xf3 should be winning for White.

45...♗a4!! 0-1

Suddenly there is absolutely no defence to ...♖d1 mate (that pawn on f4 plays a crucial role!).

Bologan-Gipslis
Ostrava 1993

In this roughly level endgame Black played the plausible

44...♘e3??

which allowed White to display the

power of his rooks:

45 ♘g5+!! fxg5 46 ♖b7+ ♔g8 47 ♖a8+ and it's mate next move.

Exercises

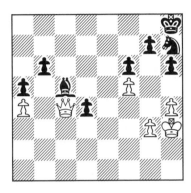

Exercise 5.1 White to play

Can White utilise his material advantage to break through in this ending?

Exercise 5.2 Black to play

Can Black get away with grabbing the pawn on e4?

CHAPTER SIX

Rampant Rooks

In *Simple Chess* I looked at various aspects of rook play, including the control of open and half-open files plus the idea of 'rook lifts'. In this final chapter I would like to expand a little by looking at less obvious features of rook play. First of all, I would like to develop the theme of open files to include the importance of outposts, while secondly I want to take a look of the growing importance of rooks being activated on their 'home files' (the a- and h-files). This idea works both with attacks and also in restraint (see below).

Outpost on an open file

In the battle for control of an open file, possession of an outpost on that file can constitute a major advantage. The rook can nestle into the outpost and this may prepare a doubling or even a trebling) of the major pieces on that file. This outpost can be particularly effective if it is supported by one, or preferably, two pawns. Here's a 'skeleton' case of this theme at work.

(see following diagram)

If it were White's move in the above diagram he should certainly play 1 ♖c5!, making full use of the outpost on c5. Black is then faced with a difficult decision. If he does nothing, then White will continue to increase the pressure on the open c-file with moves such as ♖ec1 and ♕c3. However, capturing on c5 allows White to obtain a very powerful protected passed pawn and put Black firmly on the defensive. White would probably recapture with bxc5, leaving Black's b-pawn vulnerable to attack along the open b-file. Likewise, if it were Black to move, he could play 1...♖c4!.

In the following example White makes

very good use of the outpost on the open file.

Geller-Naranja
Palma de Mallorca 1970
Petroff Defence

1 e4 e5 2 ♘f3 ♘f6 3 d4 ♘xe4 4 ♗d3 d5 5 ♘xe5 ♗d6 6 0-0 0-0 7 c4 ♘c6 8 ♘xc6 bxc6 9 c5 ♗e7 10 ♘d2 ♘xd2 11 ♗xd2 ♗f6 12 ♗c3 a5 13 ♗c2 ♕d7 14 h3 g6 15 ♖e1 ♗g7 16 ♗a4 ♖a6 17 ♕f3 ♕d8 18 ♖e2 ♗d7 19 ♖ae1 f5 20 ♕f4 ♗f6 21 ♕d2 ♖a7 22 ♕d3 ♖e8 23 ♖xe8+ ♗xe8 24 ♗d2 ♗d7 25 ♗f4 ♕f8

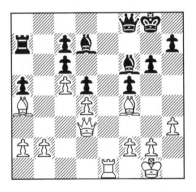

White's control of the open file, more active pieces and superior pawn structure should add up to a decisive advantage. At the moment there is no entry point for the rook on the e-file, but crucially White does possess an important outpost on e5.

26 ♗e5!

Good, logical play. The white bishop occupies the dominating post and induces a trade. With the dark-squared bishops off the board, White's rook has more penetration squares on the e-file.

26...♗xe5 27 ♖xe5 ♖a8 28 f4

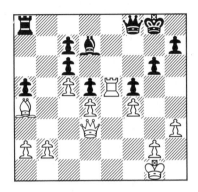

Cementing the rook's position in anticipation of ...♖e8.

28...♖e8 29 ♕e3 ♔f7

At the moment Black has all the threats covered, but Geller's next plan is to induce another exchange on e5.

30 ♔h2 ♕h8 31 ♕d2

I prefer the more forcing 31 ♕e1, after which 31...♖xe5 (31...♖a8? loses to 32 ♖e7+) 32 fxe5 ♕a8 33 ♕h4 ♔g8 34 ♕f6 ♕f8 transposes to the game. After the text move it's possible that Black could try to grovel with 31...♖a8 32 ♕e1 ♕f6.

31...♖xe5 32 fxe5

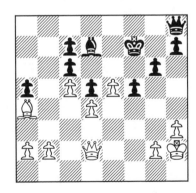

The advantage of the controlling the open file and possession of an outpost has been converted to a new plus: a protected passed pawn. Furthermore, White's last move provides a new avenue for the white queen into Black's position.

32...♕a8 33 ♕g5! ♕e8 34 ♕f6+ ♔g8 35 ♔g3! ♕f8 36 ♔f4!

Excellent technique from Geller. Black is allowed to trade queens, but only at a cost of allowing White a passed pawn further down the board that can be protected by the king.

36...♕xf6?

Black accepts, but after this he is totally lost. The only possible way to stay in the game is with 36...♕h6+.

37 exf6 h6 38 ♔e5 ♔f7 39 ♗c2 ♗c8 40 ♗d3 h5

More pawns on light squares, but Black really has no choice as otherwise White could play h3-h4-h5.

41 h4 ♗b7 42 g3 ♗c8 43 a3! 1-0

Black had seen enough and decided to throw in the towel. One winning line runs 43 a3 ♗d7 (or 43...♗b7 44 b4 axb4 45 axb4 ♗c8 46 b5 ♗b7 47 b6!, giving the king access to d6) 44 b4 axb4 45 axb4 ♔f8 46 ♗a6! ♔f7 47 ♗b7 ♔f8 48 b5! cxb5 49 ♗xd5 b4 50 ♗b3 ♗e8 51 d5 ♗f7 52 c6 (threatening d6!) 52...♗e8 53 d6 ♗xc6 54 dxc7 ♗b7 55 ♔d6 ♗c8 56 ♗e6 ♗a6 57 ♔c5.

In some cases the rook can go ahead

and occupy the outpost even if this square is guarded by a minor piece. The sacrifice of the 'exchange' may be a small price to pay if a powerful protected passed pawn is obtained. The example below is a rather lopsided case of this.

Anand-Kasparov
PCA World Ch'ship (Game 9),
New York 1995

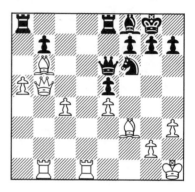

Anand, already with the advantage, leapt into the outpost with

27 ♖d5!

Despite the power of the rook on this square and the option of White to double rooks on the d-file, Black should probably sit tight. After all, the further entry squares d6, d7 and d8 are all well covered. Unfortunately for him, Kasparov couldn't resist – 'doing nothing' and sitting on a disadvantage is not one of his greater strengths.

27...♘xd5??

The double question mark was given by Anand in his notes to *Chess Informant*. White now obtains a monster of a passed pawn.

28 exd5 ♕g6 29 c5 e4

Perhaps Kasparov had been banking on obtaining enough counterplay through the advance of this pawn, but Anand demonstrates that this is not the case.

30 ♗e2 ♖e5 31 ♕d7! ♖g5 32 ♖g1 e3 33 d6

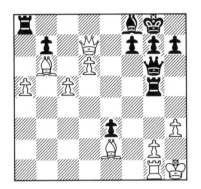

White is simply going to capture on b7, leaving him with three massive pawns. An attempt to prevent this with 33...♕e4 fails to 34 ♗f3.

33...♖g3 34 ♕xb7 ♕e6

One last cheapo – Black hopes to play ...♖xh3+!.

35 ♔h2! 1-0

35...♖e8 loses to 36 d7, while following 36...♕e5 White can calmly capture on a8 as Black has no useful discovered check.

There doesn't necessarily have to be a pawn covering the outpost for there to be a successful occupation. Take a look at the following game, in which the theme of 'good' bishop against 'bad' bishop is also very much in evidence.

Nielsen-Rozentalis

Bundesliga 2001

Nimzo-Indian Defence

1 c4 ♘f6 2 ♘c3 e6 3 ♘f3 ♗b4 4 ♕c2 0-0 5 a3 ♗xc3 6 ♕xc3 b6 7 e3 ♗b7 8 ♗e2 d6 9 0-0 ♘e4 10 ♕c2 ♘g5 11 ♘xg5 ♕xg5 12 f3 e5 13 d4 exd4 14 exd4 ♕f6 15 ♗e3 ♖e8 16 ♕d2 d5 17 ♗g5 ♕e6 18 ♖fe1 ♘c6 19 c5 ♕g6 20 ♗d3 f5 21 ♗b5 a6 22 ♗a4 b5 23 ♗b3 ♘xd4 24 ♕xd4 ♕xg5

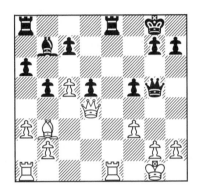

25 ♖e5!!

A wonderful example of non-stereotyped play from White. By refusing to recapture on d5 White has certainly saddled Black with a bad bishop. More importantly, though, White's last move is a high-class demonstration of how to dominate a file by using an outpost. I suspect that Black is actually already in big trouble here.

25...c6 26 ♖ae1 ♖xe5 27 ♕xe5 ♖f8 28 ♕e6+

Keeping things very much under control. There's no need to rush when your position has so many long-term positives. In contrast, 28 ♕c7? ♕d2! (Wells) gives Black undeserved counterplay.

28...♖f7 29 ♕e8+ ♖f8 30 ♕e6+ ♖f7 31 ♕d6! h6 32 ♖e8+ ♔h7 33 f4!

This is a further restriction of Black's queen.

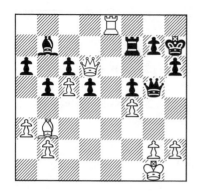

33...♕g4

Alternatives demonstrate how miserable Black's position has become:

a) 33...♕h4 34 ♕e6 ♕h5 35 h3!, when the threat of g2-g4 is absolutely decisive (...♕g6 can always be met by ♖h8+!).

b) 33...♕f6 34 ♕xf6! ♖xf6 35 ♖e7 ♗a8 36 ♔f2 when despite the extra pawn the endgame is truly grim for Black, who can hardly move.

34 h3 ♕g3

This loses. Black's only chance is with the admittedly depressing line 34...♕h4 35 ♕e6 ♕f6 36 ♕xf6 ♖xf6, leading to an endgame very similar to the one described in note 'b' to Black's 33rd move. Perhaps Rozentalis saw this but preferred to be put out of his misery!

35 ♕e6

Now White's major pieces finally smoke out the black king.

35...♖f6 36 ♕g8+ ♔g6 37 ♖e7 ♔h5 38 ♗d1+ ♔h4 39 ♖xg7 1-0

A likely finish is 39...♕e1+ 40 ♔h2 ♕xd1 41 g3+ ♔h5 42 ♖g5+! hxg5 43 ♕xg5 mate.

Working from home

Advice to beginners usually includes such pearls of wisdom as 'centralise your rooks' and it's clear that in the majority of cases rooks normally move away from their original squares to seek open or half-open files. Nevertheless, I've noticed that in modern chess there has been a growing tendency for rooks to be activated on their 'home' files (the a- and h-files) and I would like to take a look at a few examples of that here.

The most obvious and 'classical' way of utilising a rook on its own file is by actually opening this file, via a pawn break or a piece exchange. We've already seen one example of how effective this can be (see page 41). Ilia Smirin's exploitation of the open a-file in the game below is also worth seeing.

Smirin-Gabdrakhmanov

Russian Team Ch'ship, Togliatti 2003

Ruy Lopez

1 e4 e5 2 ♘f3 ♘c6 3 ♗b5 a6 4 ♗a4
d6 5 c3 ♗d7 6 0-0 ♘ge7 7 d4 ♘g6
8 ♖e1 ♗e7 9 ♘bd2 h6 10 ♘f1 ♗g5
11 ♗e3 b5 12 ♗c2 ♕f6

13 a4!

In an attempt to activate the dormant
rook on a1, White strikes out on the
queenside at just the right moment. Now
Black must make a difficult decision.

13...♖b8?

I can understand Black's reluctance to
castle (he's still hoping to be able to use a
half-open h-file if White could be
tempted to capture on g5). Nevertheless,
I'm convinced that this is what Black
should have done, as now the white rook
gets to exploit the soon-to-be-opened a-
file with devastating effect.

Note that trying to keep things
blocked with 13...b4 wasn't an option on
account of 14 d5!, winning the b4-pawn.

14 axb5 axb5 15 ♖a6!

Exceptional play from Smirin – the
rook is surprisingly effective on this rank.
The x-ray effect through to the queen
causes Black all sorts of problems.

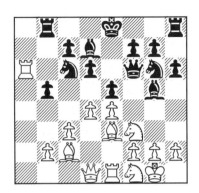

15...♘h4?

After this Black runs into big trouble.
The move 15...♖b6? was not possible
due to 16 dxe5! and ♗xb6, so Black
should probably make do with castling.

16 ♘xh4 ♗xh4 17 g3 ♗g5

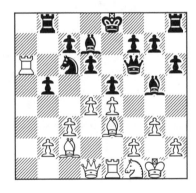

18 dxe5!

Simple and yet very effective. The
rook's presence along the sixth rank is
very much starting to be felt.

18...♘xe5

This just loses material, but the alternative 18...dxe5 leaves Black in some
discomfort after the move 19 ♗b3!, intending to increase the pressure with
either ♗d5 or ♕d5. The attempt to kick
out the rook from its post on a6 with
19...♗c8 fails tactically to 20 ♗xf7+!

when White wins a pawn after either 20...♛xf7 21 ♖xc6 or 20...♚xf7 21 ♛d5+ ♛e6 22 ♖xc6.

19 f4 ♗g4 20 fxe5 ♗xd1 21 exf6 ♗xc2 22 fxg7 ♖g8 23 e5! d5 24 h4 ♗e7 25 ♗xh6

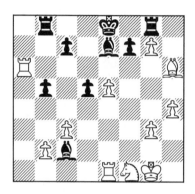

The smoke has cleared leaving White with an easily winning endgame.

25...b4 26 ♘e3 ♗e4 27 ♘g4 bxc3 28 bxc3 ♗c5+ 29 ♘e3 d4 30 cxd4 ♗xd4 31 ♖a4 c5 32 ♖xd4 cxd4 33 ♘g4 ♗f5 34 ♘f6+ ♚e7 35 g4 ♗c2 36 ♖a1 d3 37 ♚f2 ♖gd8 38 ♗g5 ♚e6 39 ♖a6+ ♚xe5 40 ♚e3 ♖b4 41 ♘d7+ 1-0

Next up we have an enlightening piece of imaginative thinking in a particularly topical line of the Ruy Lopez.

1 e4 e5 2 ♘f3 ♘c6 3 ♗b5 a6 4 ♗a4 ♘f6 5 0-0 b5 6 ♗b3 ♗c5 7 a4 ♖b8 8 c3 d6 9 d4 ♗b6 10 ♘a3 0-0 11 axb5 axb5 12 ♘xb5 exd4 13 cxd4 ♗g4

Despite the theory being very recent, this position, arising from what is generally known as the New Archangel Variation, has already been reached many times. Black has sacrificed a pawn but has definite compensation in the form of pressure on both central pawns and the possibility of tactics against White's slightly vulnerable minor pieces on the half-open b-file.

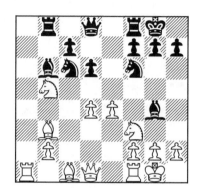

What is interesting about this is how the theory has developed. Initial attempts by White players included the obvious tries 14 ♖e1, 14 ♗c2, 14 ♗e3 and 14 ♗g5. However, after resources were found for Black in each of these lines, White players began looking at less dogmatic ideas and in the game Bologan-Tkachiev, Enghien les Bains 1999 White played the move **14 ♖a4!** (although apparently this move is the brainchild of Peter Svidler). I've given the exclamation mark for imagination rather than for the objective merits of the move. I don't want to try to solve this position although initial feelings suggest this is at least as good as White's other tries. I will just point out that 14...♘xe4? fails to 15 ♗d5 ♛e8 16 ♛c2 ♘e7 17 ♗xe4 ♛xb5 18 ♗xh7+ ♚h8 19 ♗e4, so Black players have concentrated their efforts on 14...♖e8 and 14...♛e8!?. What is particularly interesting is the fact that 14 ♖a4 was only considered after all the more obvious possibilities were exhausted (perhaps this is a case of players being conditioned to centralise rooks). One further point is that since 14 ♖a4 came to the fore, the even less obvious 14 ♖a3!? has been tried (I believe Anand was the first to play this).

Examples like this are all well and good, but what happens if your opponent doesn't allow you to open the rook's file. In this case there is sometimes still a solution, even if it does superficially look like a beginner's move! Look at Movsesian's play in the following example.

Timman-Movsesian
Malmö 1999
Sicilian Defence

1 e4 c5 2 ♘f3 e6 3 d4 cxd4 4 ♘xd4 ♘c6 5 ♘c3 ♕c7 6 ♗e3 a6 7 ♗d3 ♘f6 8 0-0 h5!?

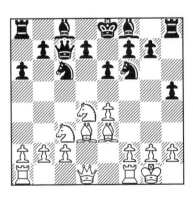

Classical players would be dismayed by this move, but this game shows that there is some point to Black's play (it's not just a cheap threat of ...♘g4). For the record, 'normal' moves include 8...b5, 8...♗d6, 8...♘e5 and 8...♘xd4.

9 h3 b5 10 ♘xc6 ♕xc6 11 a3 ♗b7

12 ♖e1 ♗d6 13 ♗d4 e5 14 ♗e3 ♗c5 15 ♕d2 ♖c8 16 ♗xc5 ♕xc5 17 ♕g5 ♔f8!

A revealing moment, as Movsesian demonstrates that he has no intention of connecting the rooks via castling. Indeed, 17...0-0? would be a mistake that would leave the h-pawn looking a bit silly on h5. White could try to exploit this by going on an immediate attack with 18 ♖e3!.

18 ♖ad1 h4!

The justification of Black's previous play. Now Black plans to activate the rook via h5! **19 ♗f1 ♖h5 20 ♕d2 ♗c6 21 b4 ♕e7 22 ♘d5?!**

This move eases Black's task by activating the c8-rook and giving the other one the f5-square. As an improvement, Movsesian suggests keeping the status quo with 22 ♕e3.

22...♗xd5 23 exd5 ♕d6

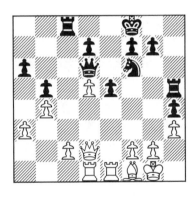

24 ♗e2?

Movsesian doesn't comment on this move but I don't like it, as after this Black reaches a winning position without much effort. Good or bad, White has to try something quickly on the queenside, although I do admit the variations seem to favour Black, for example:

a) 24 a4 e4! 25 axb5 ♖xd5 26 ♕c1 axb5 27 ♗xb5 ♕xb4 28 ♖xd5 ♘xd5 29 ♗xd7 ♖xc2 30 ♕xc2 ♕xe1+ 31 ♔h2 ♕c3 with a clear advantage (Movsesian).

b) 24 c4!? (this looks absolutely critical) 24...bxc4 25 ♖c1 ♕xd5 26 ♕xd5 ♘xd5 27 ♗xc4 ♘f4 28 ♗xa6 ♖xc1 29 ♖xc1 ♖g5, when Black has the better of a very complex ending. One possible continuation, mainly 'Fritz generated', certainly not forced but giving a flavour of the situation, runs 30 ♖c8+ ♔e7 31 ♗b7 d5 32 a4 ♖xg2+ 33 ♔h1 ♖xf2 34 a5 ♖f3! (showing remarkable indifference towards White's a-pawn racing up the board) 35 a6 ♖xh3+ 36 ♔g1 ♖a3 37 b5 g5! 38 b6 g4 39 a7 ♖a1+ 40 ♔f2 g3+ 41 ♔f3 g2 42 ♖g8 h3 43 ♗a6 h2 44 a8♕ ♖f1+ 45 ♔e3 g1♕+ and Black mates!

24...♖f5 25 ♗f3 ♖c4 26 ♗e2 ♖c8

26...♖xf2 looks tempting, but 27 ♕e3 ♖cf4 28 ♕c5! ♕xc5 gives White counterplay.

27 ♗f3 ♖f4

Black's strategy beginning with 8...h5!? has turned out to be a great success. Just look at the activity of the black rooks.

28 ♕e3 e4 29 ♖d4 ♖xc2 30 ♗xe4 ♖cxf2

Just as Black reaches a winning posi-

tion, the rooks are finally connected for the first time. Classicists may approve after all!

31 ♖c1

31 ♕xf2 loses after 31...♖xf2 32 ♔xf2 ♕b6 33 ♔e3 ♘xe4! 34 ♔xe4 ♕g6+ 35 ♔f3 ♕g3+ 36 ♔e2 ♕e5+, when Black wins one of the rooks.

31...♕e5! 32 ♖c8+ ♘e8 33 ♖d1 f5 34 ♕c5+ d6 35 ♖xe8+ ♔xe8 36 ♕c8+ ♔f7 0-1

I couldn't resist including the following game, which I first came across when working on my Benoni website at *ChessPublishing.com*. I remember being incredibly impressed by Greenfeld's original way of development. In particular, he somehow manages to activate both his rooks on their original squares!

Hasidovski-Greenfeld
Israeli League, Ramat Aviv 2000
Irregular Benoni

1 d4 ♘f6 2 ♘f3 c5 3 d5 b5 4 ♗g5 ♘e4 5 ♗h4 ♗b7 6 ♕d3 f5 7 ♘bd2 c4 8 ♕d4 ♘a6

Already the opening suggests something different from the norm.

9 0-0-0

If now 9 ♘xe4 fxe4 10 ♕xe4 ♘b4 11 0-0-0 then 11...♕a5 looks reasonable enough for Black, especially as 12 a3 can be answered by 12...♘xd5! 13 ♖xd5? e6!.

9...♘b4 10 ♘xe4 fxe4 11 ♘g5 ♕b6! 12 ♕xe4 ♘xa2+ 13 ♔b1 ♘b4

We've reached a somewhat unusual position, in which only one central pawn (White's d-pawn) has actually moved. White can try and attack Black's weakened kingside, while Black attempts to do the same on the other wing.

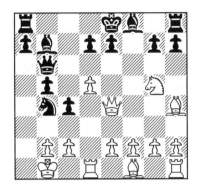

14 c3

14 ♘xh7 ♘xd5 15 ♖xd5 ♖xh7 16 ♕xh7 ♗xd5 17 e4 ♗f7 is an amusing line, which looks roughly level.

14...h6!

Forcing an activation of one of the rooks. The immediate 14...♘xd5? fails to 15 ♖xd5 e6 16 ♘xh7!, but now 15 ♘f3 can be answered by 15...♘xd5!.

15 cxb4 hxg5 16 ♗xg5 a5!

A second rook is activated. Black is still a pawn down, but this is rather irrelevant when he has such a raging attack.

17 ♗e3 ♕e6!!

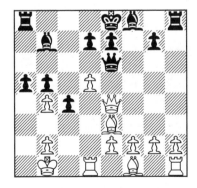

A shocking move, which takes the game up to a different level.

18 ♕xe6

18 dxe6 ♗xe4+ 19 ♔c1 dxe6 is also better for Black.

18...dxe6 19 bxa5 exd5 20 ♗b6 e5 21 e3 ♖h6!

One of the main ideas behind this only becomes apparent in three moves time. White still has the extra pawn, but Black is extremely active, with an impressive pawn umbrella on the queenside. One idea Black has is to simply round up the a5-pawn with ...♗f8-b4xa5.

22 ♗e2 d4!

This is even stronger than 22...♗b4.

23 exd4

Now Black has a winning combination.

23...♗e4+! 24 ♔c1

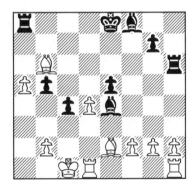

24...♖xb6!!

Not that difficult to see, but very pleasing nevertheless. And Greenfeld obviously had this idea in mind with 21...♖h6!.

25 axb6 ♗b4

A complete triumph for the rooks and bishops – suddenly White cannot avoid mate.

26 b3 ♗c3 0-1

This game definitely leaves quite an impression!

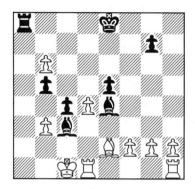

Rooks and restraint

The final two games of this chapter once again see rooks working on their home files, although this time the theme is restraint. In fact both games open with the main line of the Berlin Defence, in which, given that Black's king is stuck in the centre for long periods, he very much relies on activating his rooks on the a- and h-files.

Kasparov-Kramnik

BGN World Ch'ship (Game 1),
London 2000
Ruy Lopez

1 e4 e5 2 ♘f3 ♘c6 3 ♗b5 ♘f6 4 0-0 ♘xe4 5 d4 ♘d6 6 ♗xc6 dxc6 7 dxe5 ♘f5 8 ♕xd8+ ♔xd8 9 ♘c3 ♗d7 10 b3 h6 11 ♗b2 ♔c8 12 h3 b6 13 ♖ad1 ♘e7 14 ♘e2 ♘g6 15 ♘e1

A typical position from this opening. Kasparov's slow manoeuvring with his knights is aimed at getting into position for an eventual advance of the kingside pawn majority. Now Kramnik puts into a place a restraining method very much in the style of Nimzowitsch.

15...h5!

Preventing g2-g4 and making White think twice about arranging this move due to the activation of the h8-rook.

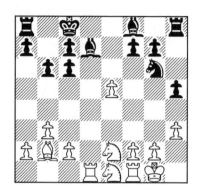

16 ♘d3 c5

Black's plan isn't entirely defensive. This move plans ideas such as ...♗e6 followed by ...c5-c4, straightening out his own pawn majority. Kasparov prevents this with his very next move.

17 c4 a5!

Now Black plans activity down the a-file, so Kasparov correctly prevents this.

18 a4!

After 18 ♘df4 ♘xf4 19 ♘xf4 a4! 20 ♖d2 axb3 21 axb3 ♗f5 22 ♖fd1 ♔b7 23 ♖d8 ♗e7! (Kramnik) Black coordinates just in time.

18...h4!

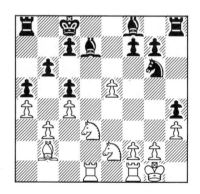

We've already seen this idea. On this occasion Black pretty much rules out the possibility of g2-g4, as after the en passant White's kingside pawns would be severely compromised.

19 ♘c3

Or 19 ♘df4 ♘xf4 20 ♘xf4 ♗f5 (threatening ...♗c2, highlighting a problem with a2-a4) 21 ♖d2 ♗e7 (threatening ...♗g5) 22 ♘d5 ♖e8! and Black will continue with ...♔b7 etc. If White exchanges on e7, then the ending involving opposite-coloured bishops may well favour Black. White's kingside majority is easily held on the light squares, while in a pure bishop ending the weakness at b3 is glaring.

19...♗e6

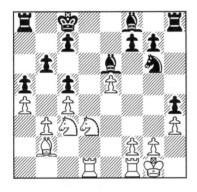

20 ♘d5

White can play f4 easily enough but, crucially, being able to push the pawn to f5 is impossible; for example, 20 f4 ♘e7 and Black can always follow up with ...g6 and ...♖h5!.

20...♔b7 21 ♘e3!

Now f2-f4-f5 is a threat that Black must take seriously.

21...♖h5!

The most accurate move. 21...♘e7 22 ♘f4! (Kramnik) is annoying for Black,

who wants to keep his light-squared bishop. Now Black is ready to meet f2-f4 with ...♘e7!, after which there is no longer the possibility of f5 (or ♘f4 for that matter).

22 ♗c3 ♖e8 23 ♖d2 ♔c8 24 f4

Finally Kasparov sees that there is nothing better to do.

24...♘e7! 25 ♘f2 ♘f5

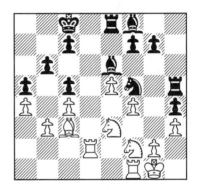

and a draw was agreed. One possible continuation is 25...♘f5 26 ♘xf5 ♗xf5 27 ♘g4 ♗e7 28 ♘e3 ♗e6 29 ♔h2 (29 f5? runs into 29...♗g5) 29...g6 and Black has a perfect blockade.

Incidentally, this was the first game of their world championship match and certainly set the tone. Despite several attempts, Kasparov was unable to make any headway at all against this super-solid defence, which proved to be an inspired choice for Kramnik.

I should say that Kramnik was certainly not the first to prove the viability of this line. The Berlin Defence was a great favourite of Tony Miles, who had astonishing success with it, while the German grandmaster Rustem Dautov also won some very nice games with it. More recently the Hungarian GM Zoltan

Almasi has displayed many new defensive resources for Black. Despite the fact that the following game again 'only' ends in a draw, I was still very impressed with Black's play. In games like this it really does seem as if White is banging his head against a (Berlin) wall.

Peng Xiaomin-Z.Almasi
Groningen 1997
Ruy Lopez

1 e4 e5 2 ♘f3 ♘c6 3 ♗b5 ♘f6 4 0-0 ♘xe4 5 d4 ♘d6 6 ♗xc6 dxc6 7 dxe5 ♘f5 8 ♕xd8+ ♔xd8 9 ♖d1+ ♔e8 10 ♘c3 ♘e7 11 ♘d4 ♘g6 12 ♘e4 ♗e7 13 f4 ♗g4 14 ♖d3 ♖d8 15 h3 ♗d7 16 ♗e3 c5 17 ♘e2 b6 18 c4

18...h5!

Again we see this move. Note that Almasi's knight manoeuvre ...♘f5-e7-g6 leaves it well placed on this square: even if White can protect the f5-square in readiness for f4-f5, he still has to worry about the defence of the e5-pawn.

19 ♖ad1 h4! 20 ♘2c3 ♗f5 21 ♔f2?!

A natural-looking move, but after this White actually has to play accurately to equalise. As an alternative, Peng Xiaomin

suggests the imaginative 21 ♖d5! ♗e6 22 ♘b5! ♗xd5 23 cxd5, when White certainly has compensation for the material deficit.

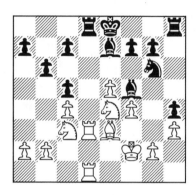

21...♖xd3 22 ♖xd3 ♖h5!

Giving Black further options.

23 b3

23 g4? hxg3+ 24 ♘xg3 doesn't work due to 24...♗h4!.

23...♗xe4!?

Another possible idea is ...♘f8-e6.

24 ♘xe4 ♖f5

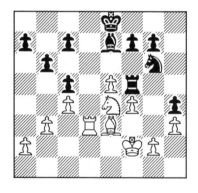

25 g3!

Black has given up his light-squared bishop but in return White is forced to compromise his pawn structure. Notice how the black rook is now very much in an active role.

25 ♔f3? loses to the obvious 25...♘xe5+, while 25 g4 fails to 25...♘xf4!.

25...hxg3+

Not 25...♘xe5? 26 ♖d5!.

26 ♔xg3 ♖h5 27 ♘c3 ♗d8!

The restraint continues. Now Black plans ...♘e7.

28 ♔g4 ♖h4+ 29 ♔g3 ♖h8 30 ♔g4

Sensibly offering a repetition of moves, which Almasi accepts. Attempts by White to continue may well prove to be risky. One instructive line given by Peng Xiaomin runs 30 ♘e4 ♘e7! 31 ♔g4 ♘g8!

when despite having all his pieces on the back rank, Black is probably better! The point is that there is no good way to prevent a blockade with ...♘h6-f5, as 32 f5 drops a pawn to 32...♖h4+.

30...♖h4+ 31 ♔g3 ♖h8 32 ♔g4 ♖h4+ 33 ♔g3 ♖h8 ½-½

Exercises

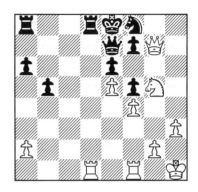

Exercise 6.1 White to play

Can you spot how White makes use of the open d-file? (I should mention that Black's position is even worse than it looks – he's already moved his king so castling is out of the question.

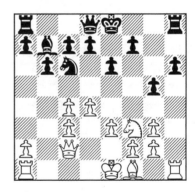

Exercise 6.2 White to play

Can you see an effective way forward for White?

CHAPTER SEVEN

Solutions to Exercises

Exercise 1.1
Short-Gelfand
3rd match game, Brussels 1991
Sicilian Defence

**(1 e4 c5 2 ♘c3 d6 3 f4 ♘c6 4 ♘f3
g6 5 ♗c4 ♗g7 6 0-0 e6 7 d3 ♘ge7
8 ♕e1 ♘d4 9 ♘xd4 cxd4 10 ♘e2
0-0 11 ♗b3 ♘c6 12 ♗d2 d5 13 e5
f6 14 exf6 ♗xf6)**

The passively placed knight would
much prefer to be on f3, where it still
hits the d4-pawn, controls the important
e5-square and also has the aggressive
possibility of moving on to g5. At first it
seems difficult for White to arrange this
piece set-up, but Short just uses a little
imagination...
15 ♔h1!

(see following diagram)

So easy once you see it – the knight
will reappear via g1. It's amazing how
often the back rank can be used to improve a piece's position.
**15...a5 16 a4 ♕d6 17 ♘g1 ♗d7 18
♘f3**

It's quite instructive how the knight
now plays an instrumental role in White
winning the game.

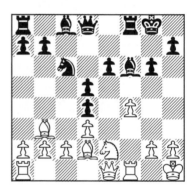

18...♘b4?!

Overlooking a tactical idea that forces
this knight to retreat back to c6. After
18...♖ae8 or 18...b6 Black wouldn't have
many problems.
**19 ♕f2! ♕c5 20 ♗c3! ♘c6 21 ♖ae1
b6 22 ♗d2 ♘b4?! 23 ♕g3 b5 24 f5!
exf5 25 ♘e5 ♗e8 26 axb5 ♕xb5 27
♖xf5 ♔h8 28 ♖xf6!**

Eliminating the defences.
**28...♖xf6 29 ♘g4 ♖f5 30 ♘h6 ♖h5
31 ♕f4 1-0**

Exercise 1.2
Djuric-Emms
Islington 1993

29 ♗xe5!

Forcing the black rook onto an inconvenient square. 29 e4? ♖d4! would even be good for Black!

29...♖xe5 30 e4!

Preventing ...♖d5 and leaving the rook on e5 very awkwardly placed. It's true that for the moment it ties down White's own rook to the defence of c5, but White has the simple plan of ♔f3-e3-d4 followed by ♖a4. With Black's rook out of the game, White would be left with a decisive power play.

30...f5 31 f3!

The most important thing is to keep Black's rook boxed in. Note that only Black has winning chances after 31 f4?? ♖xe4 32 ♖xe4 fxe4 33 ♔f2 ♔f7 34 ♔e3 ♔e6 35 ♔xe4 a5.

31...g5?

Panic. Logically, my best chance to save the game was to re-activate my poorly placed rook via 31...fxe4 32 fxe4 ♖e6! 33 ♔f3 ♖f6+ 34 ♔e3 ♖f1.

32 hxg5 fxe4 33 f4!

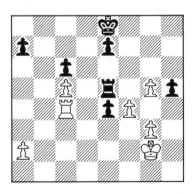

Now Black's pawns are weak and

White has a very strong pawn phalanx on the kingside. The rest of the game is pretty straightforward.

33...♖d5 34 ♖xe4 ♖xc5 35 g6 ♔f8 36 g7+ ♔g8 37 ♖e7 ♖a5 38 ♔h3 ♖xa2 39 ♔h4 ♖a5 40 g4! hxg4 41 ♔xg4 ♖a1 42 ♔g5 ♖g1+ 43 ♔f6 ♔h7 44 f5 a5 45 ♔e6 a4 46 f6 a3 47 ♔f7 1-0

Exercise 1.3
Bareev-Short
Moscow (rapid) 2002
Nimzo-Indian Defence

(1 d4 ♘f6 2 c4 e6 3 ♘c3 ♗b4 4 ♕c2 d5 5 a3 ♗xc3+ 6 ♕xc3 dxc4 7 ♕xc4 b6 8 ♘f3 ♗a6)

White's queen is attacked and it needs to find a suitable home. After the obvious 9 ♕c2 Black can complete his development in natural fashion with 9...♘bd7 followed by ...0-0 and perhaps ...c7-c5. Instead of this, Bareev produces an important finesse.

9 ♕a4+!

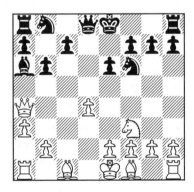

A deceptively powerful idea: White lures Black into making a move that he doesn't really want to make, before retreating the queen back its favoured home at c2.

9...♕d7

Other moves also have drawbacks. 9...b5? 10 ♕c2 suddenly makes the bishop on a6 look silly, while the stronger 9...c6 still leaves Black with problems of how to develop the b8-knight without losing the c6-pawn.

10 ♕c2

A job well done, the white queen returns to safety. Black's queen has been lured to the d7-square and this interferes with his desired scheme of development – it's the b8-knight that really covets this square. Instead it has to make do with second best.

10...♘c6

In his notes to this game in *Chess Informant* Bareev suggests that Black should make use of the 'extra' tempo with 10...♕c6, but I still prefer White's position after 11 ♕xc6+ ♘xc6 12 ♗f4 ♘d5 13 ♗g3, intending ♖c1.

11 ♗g5!

Making way so that the a1-rook can slot nicely into d1. Now 11...♘xd4 leads to a very favourable ending for White after 12 ♘xd4 ♕xd4 13 ♕c6+ ♔e7 14 ♖d1 ♕c5 15 ♖d7+ ♔e8 16 ♕xc5! (but not 16 ♕xa8+? ♔xd7 17 ♕xh8 ♕xg5, when I prefer Black) 16...bxc5 17 ♖xc7.

11...0-0 12 ♖d1

Black is actually ahead on pieces moved, but here it is certainly a case of quality over quantity – Black's development is more clumsy than harmonious. White's plan is simply to play g2-g3, ♗g2 and 0-0 with an obvious edge. Here Black should opt for damage limitation with 12...♖fd8! 13 g3 ♗b7 14 ♗g2 ♘e7 15 ♗xf6 gxf6 16 0-0 (Bareev), but instead Short lurched into deeper trouble.

12...♖ac8? 13 ♘e5!

Of course!

13...♘xe5 14 dxe5 ♕b5

14...♘d5? simply loses a piece after 15 e4 ♗xf1 16 ♖xf1.

15 ♗xf6 gxf6 16 exf6 ♕a5+ 17 ♕c3 ♕xc3+ 18 bxc3

White has a solid extra pawn. The rest of the game is not really relevant, Bareev comfortably going on to convert his advantage into the full point.

Exercise 2.1
Wells-Jakobsen
Koeszeg 2000
Catalan Opening

(1 d4 ♘f6 2 ♘f3 d5 3 c4 e6 4 g3 dxc4 5 ♗g2 ♘c6 6 ♕a4 ♗b4+ 7 ♗d2 ♘d5 8 ♗xb4 ♘dxb4 9 0-0 ♖b8 10 ♘a3 0-0 11 ♕b5 b6 12 ♕xc4 ♕e7 13 ♖fc1 ♗a6 14 ♘b5 ♖bd8 15 a3 ♖d5 16 axb4 ♗xb5 17 ♕c3 a6 18 e3 ♖d7)

Black's fragile queenside is only being held together by the tremendous defensive bishop on b5, which simultaneously covers many of the crucial light squares such as a6 and c6. Wells overcomes this problem by making an exchange offer that Black cannot refuse.

19 ♗f1! ♗xf1 20 ♔xf1

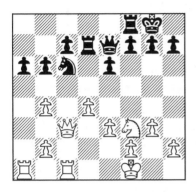

Suddenly Black's queenside is indefensible.

20...♘xb4 21 ♘e5 ♖d5 22 ♕xc7 ♕xc7 23 ♖xc7 ♖b5

23...b5 loses a pawn to 24 ♘c6!.

24 ♖b7!

Underlining the consequences of Black losing his valuable bishop. Now both ♘c4 and ♘d7 are on the agenda.

24...f6 25 ♘c4 ♖d8 26 ♖xb6 ♖xb6 27 ♘xb6

White is a safe pawn up and went on to win the game.

Exercise 2.2
Agaev-Erenburg
World Junior Ch'ship, Nakhchivan 2003

24...♘e8!

Black prepares ...♗f6 to offer an exchange to White's best minor piece – the dark-squared bishop. The bishop on e5 covers many important squares and after the exchange these will be no longer under White's control.

25 ♘g4

Unsurprisingly White tries to prevent the idea, but Black has calculated and assessed the resulting position very well.

25...h5!

Accepting a slight weakness on the kingside in return for being able to force the trade of bishops.

26 ♘e3 ♗f6! 27 ♗xf6

One point of Black's play is that 27 ♕xh5?? loses to 27...g6.

27...♘xf6 28 e5 ♘g4! 29 ♗xb7 ♕xb7 30 ♘xg4 hxg4 31 ♕xg4 ♖xd3 32 ♖xd3 ♖xd3 33 ♖d1 ♕d7 34 ♖xd3 ♕xd3

Black has the better of this queen ending due to the vulnerability of White's remaining pawns. However, I would still fancy a draw with best play. In the game, though, White makes further mistakes and Black picks up the full point.

35 ♕h4 a6 36 a4 ♕d7 37 ♕g5? ♕d1+ 38 ♔g2 ♕d4! 39 ♔g1? ♕xc4 40 ♕d8+ ♔h7 41 ♕xb6 ♕xa4 42 ♕b1+

42 ♕xc5 ♕d1+ 43 ♔g2 ♕d5+ 44 ♕xd5 exd5 45 ♔f3 a5 46 ♔e3 a4 47 ♔d3 a3 48 ♔c2 d4 and one of the pawns will promote.

42...g6 43 h4 ♕b4 44 ♕d3 c4 45 ♕f3 ♕b1+ 46 ♔g2 ♕f5 47 ♕c3 ♕e4+ 48 ♔f1 ♕d5 49 ♔e2 a5 50 ♕e3 a4 51 ♕f4 ♔g8 52 h5 ♕d3+! 53 ♔e1 gxh5 0-1

Exercise 2.3
Istratescu-Nikolaidis
European Championship, Istanbul 2003
Sicilian Defence

(1 e4 c5 2 ♘f3 d6 3 d4 ♘f6 4 ♘c3 cxd4 5 ♘xd4 a6 6 ♗g5 e6 7 f4 ♕b6 8 ♘b3 ♘bd7 9 ♕d3 ♕c7 10 a4 b6 11 ♕h3 h6 12 ♗h4 g6 13 ♗d3 ♗g7 14 0-0 0-0 15 ♔h1 ♗b7 16 ♖ae1

♖ae8 17 ♗f2 ♘h5 18 ♗e3)

18...♗xc3!

While working on my recent book *Play the Najdorf: Scheveningen Style* I was surprised how many times I came across this seemingly suicidal idea. However, I must add that Black usually had a concrete reason for giving up so much control over the dark squares on the kingside, and it wasn't just to shatter White's queenside pawns.

Of course Black isn't forced to play in this risky fashion. 18...f5!? 19 ♘d4 ♘c5, as proposed by the Israeli GM Leonid Gofshtein, is a perfectly playable alternative.

19 bxc3 f5!

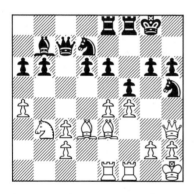

This follow-up is absolutely paramount. Unlike the Adams-Kobalija game (see page 44), White is very aggressively placed on the kingside. Black has no time to try to patch up the dark squares because White is simply threatening to blow him away with f4-f5!. So Black prevents this possibility and at the same time fights for the initiative and some light-squared control (...♗xc3 did, after all, remove a defender of both d5 and e4). This is again dissimilar to the Adams-Kobalija example, when Black es-

sentially adopted a solid, passive role.

20 e5!?

Unsurprisingly White tries to open things up for his bishop on e3. Following 20 exf5 exf5 Black's bishop on b7 comes alive, and he can secure further counterplay with ...♘d7-e4.

20...dxe5 21 fxe5 ♘xe5 22 ♗e2

White can grab his pawn back with 22 ♗xh6?! but then 22...♖f7 followed by ...♖h7! puts Black in the driving seat.

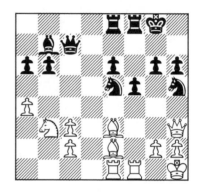

In this position Nikolaidis erred badly with 22...♕h7? (I don't understand this move at all) 23 ♗xb6 ♘f6 24 ♗c5 ♘e4? 25 ♗xf8 ♖xf8 26 ♗d3 ♘g5 27 ♕g3 ♘d7 28 ♕c7 and White soon won. However, after the consistent 22...f4!, using Black's kingside pawn majority to keep the initiative, I quite like Black's position, and variations seem to back up this assessment. For example:

a) 23 ♗d2 f3 24 gxf3 ♘f4 25 ♗xf4 ♖xf4 (Gofshtein) is good for Black.

b) 23 ♗d4 f3 24 gxf3 ♘f4 25 ♕xh6 ♖e7!? (Gofshtein's 25...♘xe2 also looks good) 26 ♘d2 ♖h7 27 ♕g5 ♖xh2+!! 28 ♔xh2 ♕h7+ 29 ♔g1 ♘h3+ and wins.

c) 23 ♗xh5 fxe3 24 ♕g3 ♖f5 25 ♗f3 (or 25 ♖xf5 exf5 26 ♗xg6? f4! 27 ♕xf4 ♕c6!) 25...♖g5 26 ♕f4 ♗xf3 27 gxf3

♕xc3 28 ♕xe3 ♕xc2 29 ♖e2 ♕c6 with advantage.

d) 23 ♗xb6 (probably best) 23...♕xb6 24 ♗xh5 ♖f5 25 ♗d1 ♖g5 with an edge for Black in a complex position.

Exercise 2.4
Emms-Jackson
Walsall 1992

I remember at the time feeling quite pleased with what I'd viewed as a non-stereotyped move.

26 ♖b1!

I figured that in the long run, my intended attack on Black's king would have a far greater chance of succeeding if I had two rooks in my weaponry instead of one. Giving up the a-file is a small price to pay for maintaining both rooks, especially as Black really has no good way to exploit this.

26...♖a7 27 g3 ♘g6 28 ♔g2 ♖ea8 29 ♗d2!

Preventing Black from trading a rook with ...♖a1!.

29...♕d8 30 ♘f5 ♗e8 31 ♖h1 ♘e7 32 ♘e3! ♘c8 33 ♕e2 ♘b6 34 f4 f6 35 ♖bf1!

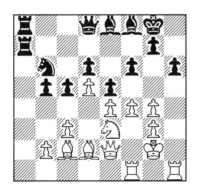

Finally we are beginning to see the

fruits of my decision to keep both rooks. Now my plan was simply to blast open the f- and h-files with g4-g5.

35...c4 36 ♘f5 ♘a4 37 ♗xa4 ♖xa4 38 g5! fxg5 39 fxg5 h5 40 ♖xh5! ♗xh5?

Suicide, but admittedly Black already had a lost position.

41 ♕xh5 1-0

Exercise 3.1
Hodgson-Psakhis
Metz 1994

Having completed the early trade, Black sets out his stall on the kingside and prepares to continue in 'Grand Prix Attack' fashion with ...♘f6 and ...0-0 with a comfortable position. Hodgson's next move puts a hefty spanner in the works.

6 c5!

I believe this imaginative sacrifice was a novelty at the time. It's certainly deemed dangerous enough that Black often plays the less committal 5...♘c6 nowadays. The point of the move is that Black can no longer avoid an opening of the position to some extent, leading to weaknesses on the dark squares. This factor certainly interests that unopposed bishop on c1.

6...dxc5

If Black allowed White to capture on d6 and recapture with the c-pawn, then White's dark-squared bishop could apply annoying pressure from the a3-square.

7 ♗a3 ♕d6 8 d4!

Consistent and entirely logical. Hodgson exploits his bishop pair and slight development lead by sacrificing another pawn to open the position up further.

8...exd4 9 cxd4 ♕xd4 10 ♕c1!

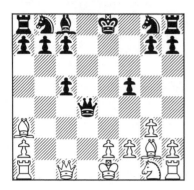

With ideas of both ♗xc5 and simply ♗b2. 10...♘d7 11 ♗b2 ♕g4 12 ♗f3 ♕g6 13 ♗h5! is a cute line that demonstrates the problems Black already finds himself in due to the power of the darksquared bishop.

10...♕f6 11 ♘h3 ♘d7 12 0-0 ♘e7 13 ♗b2 ♕f7

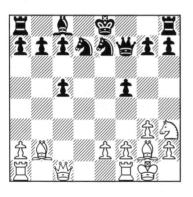

14 e4!?

In his notes to this game in *Chess Informant*, Hodgson prefers the move 14 ♕e3!, intending ♘g5; for example, 14...h6 15 ♘f4 ♘f6 16 ♕xc5 c6 17 ♗a3!, when the power of the bishop on a3 prevents Black from castling.

14...0-0 15 ♘g5 ♕g6 16 exf5 ♖xf5 17 ♖e1 ♘d5!

The best defence. 17...♕xg5 18 f4 ♕g6 19 ♖xe7 leaves Black with many problems, as 19...♖f7? loses to the simple 20 ♗d5!.

18 h4!

Intending g3-g4 followed by ♗e4.

18...♘7b6 19 ♕xc5 c6

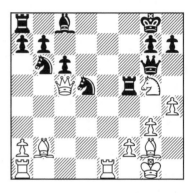

20 ♗e4?!

It's tempting to win the exchange in this way but here Hodgson shows how he could have obtained a close-to-winning advantage with the tactical sequence 20 h5! ♕xh5 (the only move; 20...♕xg5 21 ♖e8+ ♔f7 22 ♕f8 is mate) 21 g4! ♖xg5 (or 21...♕g6 22 gxf5 ♗xf5 23 ♕c1) 22 gxh5 ♗h3 23 ♔h2! ♖xg2+ 24 ♔xh3 ♘f4+ 25 ♔h4 g5+ 26 ♕xg5+! (but not 26 hxg6? ♘xg6+ 27 ♔h5 ♘f4+ when White must make do with a draw by perpetual as 28 ♔h6?? runs into 28...♖g6 mate!) 26...♖xg5 27 ♔xg5 ♘d3 28 ♖e2.

20...h6?

The incorrect move order. 20...♘a4! 21 ♕c2 ♘xb2 22 ♕xb2 h6 23 ♗xf5 ♗xf5 24 ♘f3 limits the damage, although White obviously still has some advantage.

21 ♘f3 ♘a4 22 ♕c2 ♘xb2

Finally Black has managed to rid himself of this bishop, but only at a cost of obtaining a lost position.

23 ♘d4!

An excellent move. The knight on b2 isn't going anywhere fast, so White prepares to capture on f5 with the knight rather than the bishop, leaving him in a stronger position on the light squares.

23...♘e7 24 ♘xf5 ♘xf5 25 ♕xb2 ♕f7 26 ♗c2! c5

26...♗e6? loses to 27 ♖xe6! ♕xe6 28 ♗b3.

27 ♕b5!

The threats (♖e8+, ♗b3) are mounting.

27...♗e6 28 ♕xc5 ♖c8 29 ♕xc8+! 1-0

Exercise 3.2
Emms-Speelman

Lloyds Bank Masters, London 1990

Here I came up with a rather crude-looking pair of moves that actually, on reflection, make perfect sense. At the time I'm not sure I realised why, though!

9 ♗xa6!

Not so much to double Black's pawns (the half-open b-file will offer counter-play) but to get rid of the light-squared bishop, which otherwise had an uncertain future.

9...bxa6 10 ♗h6!

and White has some advantage. Of the four remaining minor pieces that remain, the most difficult to activate is the light-squared bishop on c8.

10...♖b8 11 ♗xg7 ♔xg7 12 ♘d4 ♕e8

If 12...♖xb2 13 ♘b3! traps the rook.

13 0-0-0 e5

Here I unnecessarily complicated mat-

ters with 14 dxe6?! fxe6 15 e5!? dxe5 16 ♘b3, but instead the simple 14 ♘c6 ♖b6 15 f4! would have left White with a very promising position.

Exercise 3.3
Thipsay-Sandipan

Commonwealth Ch'ship, Mumbai 2004
Sicilian Defence

(1 e4 c5 2 ♘f3 e6 3 d4 cxd4 4 ♘xd4 ♘f6 5 ♘c3 d6 6 ♗e2 ♗e7 7 0-0 ♘c6 8 ♗e3 ♗d7 9 f4 ♘xd4 10 ♗xd4 ♗c6 11 ♗d3 0-0 12 ♔h1 ♘d7 13 ♕e2 ♕a5 14 a3 ♗f6 15 ♗xf6 ♘xf6 16 e5 dxe5 17 fxe5 ♘d7 18 ♖ae1 ♕b6 19 b4 ♕c7)

20 ♘d1!

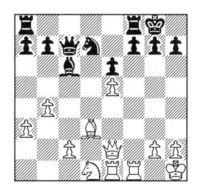

A very nice idea from Thipsay – White finds an effective way to manoeuvre his knight to the kingside without allowing an exchange or leaving his slightly vulnerable e-pawn en prise (20 ♘e4? allows the simple 20...♕xe5, but even if this were not possible, Black could eliminate the attacking piece with ...♗xe4). I should add that this plan beginning with ♘c3-d1 is not an uncommon theme in this type of Sicilian position.

20...b6

White was threatening to trap the bishop with b4-b5 and c2-c4.

21 ♘f2 a5?!

Black fails to appreciate the danger looming on the kingside with the knight's arrival. In *Chess Today* GM Ruslan Sherbakov suggests 21...♖fd8!? followed by ...♘d7-f8, covering the h7-pawn. However, even in this case White's attack still looks rather menacing to me.

22 ♘g4 axb4 23 axb4 ♖a4?

I admire Black's nonchalance towards White's attack, but unfortunately it's misplaced. The only chance to stay in the game is with 23...♕d8! 24 ♘f6+ (perhaps this should be delayed) 24...♘xf6! (24...gxf6 25 ♗xh7+! ♔xh7 26 ♕h5+ ♔g8 27 ♕g4+ ♔h7 28 ♖e3 and White mates with ♖h3) 25 exf6 g6 26 ♕e3 ♔h8 27 ♕h6 ♖g8 28 ♖e3 (threatening ♕xh7+!!) 28...♕f8 (the point of ...♕d8) 29 ♕h4 h6 and White has no immediate win.

24 ♘f6+!

A case of one step back and three steps forward. The knight's work is complete and White has a winning attack.

24...♘xf6

24...gxf6 loses as in the previous note: 25 ♗xh7+ ♔xh7 (or 25...♔h8 26 ♕h5) 26 ♕h5+ ♔g8 27 ♕g4+ ♔h8 28 ♖e3 and ♖h3 mate.

25 exf6 ♖xb4

Nothing can be done to save Black on the kingside. With Black's queen not on the d8-square, 25...g6 doesn't work due to 26 ♕e3 ♔h8 27 ♕h6 ♖g8 28 ♖e3! when there is no good defence to the threat of ♕xh7+ and ♖h3 mate.

26 ♕h5 h6 27 fxg7 ♔xg7 28 ♖xe6! 1-0

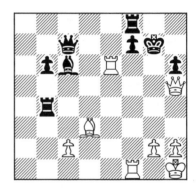

Perhaps this is the move that Black missed. Now there is no good defence (28...fxe6 loses to 29 ♕g6+ ♔h8 30 ♖xf8 mate) so Black resigned.

Exercise 3.4
Moreno-Emms
Mondariz 2000
Queen's Indian Defence

(1 d4 ♘f6 2 c4 e6 3 ♘f3 b6 4 a3 ♗a6 5 ♕c2 c5 6 d5 exd5 7 cxd5 g6 8 ♘c3 ♗g7 9 g3 0-0 10 ♗g2 d6 11 0-0 ♖e8 12 ♖e1 b5 13 e4 ♘bd7 14 ♗f4 ♕b6 15 h3 ♖ac8 16 ♗e3 ♕b7 17 ♗f1)

The strength of Black's counterplay on the queenside depends entirely upon whether he can force the move ...b5-b4. White's previous move (17 ♗f1) has prevented this idea for the moment (17...b4? loses material to the simple 18 ♗xa6 ♕xa6 19 axb3), but Black does have an unlikely solution.

17...♘b8!

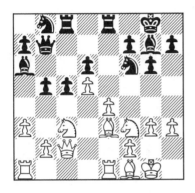

As far as I know, this was a novelty at the time and I believe it gives Black a fully playable position. It's true that this retreat makes the knight look rather ugly on the b8-square, but again it's again a case of a piece being better than it looks by performing a concrete function, that is protecting the bishop on a6. After this move White has no effective way of preventing ...b5-b4 and Black's counterplay is assured.

Previously 17...c4, intending ...♘c5 but giving away the d-square, had been played a few times before, but White was keeping the advantage; for example, 18 ♗g2 ♕b8 19 ♘d4 ♘e5 20 ♘c6 ♖xc6 (20...♘xc6 21 dxc6 ♖e6 22 ♖ad1 ♖xc6 23 e5 dxe5 24 ♗xc6 ♖xc6 25 ♕d2 was better for White in Lautier-Nisipeanu, France 2000) 21 dxc6 ♘xc6 22 f4 and Black has insufficient compensation for

the exchange, Khenkin-Almasi, Plauen 1999.

18 ♗f4

Attacking the vulnerable d6-pawn, but now Black's counter comes very quickly.

18...b4! 19 ♘d1 b3

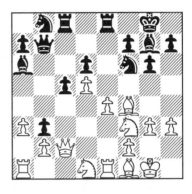

20 ♕b1?

I was very happy after I saw this move. I suspect that White should trade pawns with 20 ♗xa6 ♕xa6 (20...bxc2? 21 ♗xb7 cxd1♕ 22 ♖axd1 ♖c7 23 ♗a8! is good for White) 21 ♕xb3 ♘xe4 22 ♘c3 ♘xc3 23 bxc3 ♘d7 with a fairly level position.

20...♗xf1 21 ♔xf1 ♕a6+ 22 ♔g2 ♘bd7 23 ♘c3 c4! 24 ♗e3 ♘c5

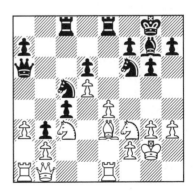

Black has gained a massive amount of space on the queenside and now White is forced to exchange on c5 in order to deal with the threat of ...♘d3.

25 ♗xc5 ♖xc5 26 ♖e3 ♘d7 27 ♕f1 ♘b6 28 ♖ae1 ♘a4 29 ♘xa4 ♕xa4 30 e5

This is White's best chance to muddy things in a grim position. Protecting the b2-pawn would just allow Black to create a decisive passed pawn with ...c4-c3.

30...♖xd5 31 ♖e4 dxe5 32 ♖xc4 ♕d7 33 ♖e3 f5 34 ♖xb3

White has won back his pawn, but now the roller on the kingside should win for Black.

34...e4 35 ♘e1 ♖d2 36 ♖c2

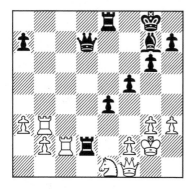

36...h5?

My intention was to play the move 36...e3! but I thought I saw a problem with 37 ♕c4+ ♕f7 (37...♔h8 38 ♖xe3 ♖xe3 39 ♖xd2 ♕xd2 40 ♕c8+ wins for White) 38 ♕xf7+ ♔xf7 39 ♖xe3 (39 ♖c7+ ♔g8 40 ♖xa7 ♖xf2+ 41 ♔g1 ♗d4 42 ♖d7 e2 wins for Black). However, I missed that after 39...♖xe3 40 ♖xd2 I have the simple 40...♖xe1 leaving me a piece up.

37 ♕c4+?

My opponent falters in time trouble. 37 ♕a6! would have put White right back in the game.

37...♔h7 38 ♖xd2 ♕xd2 39 ♘c2 h4 40 gxh4? f4 41 h5

Or 41 ♖b7 e3 42 ♕f7 ♕xf2+ 43 ♔h1 ♕f3+ 44 ♔h2 ♕e2+ 45 ♔h1 ♕d1+ and Black wins.

41...f3+ 42 ♔f1 ♕c1+ 0-1

Exercise 4.1
N.Pert-Iordachescu
Isle of Man 2003
Queen's Indian Defence

(1 d4 ♘f6 2 ♘f3 e6 3 c4 b6 4 a3 c5 5 d5 ♗a6 6 ♕c2 exd5 7 cxd5 g6 8 ♗f4 d6 9 ♘c3 ♗g7 10 ♕a4+ b5!? 11 ♘xb5 0-0 12 ♘c3 ♕b6) 13 ♕c2?!

After collecting a pawn sacrifice in the opening, Nicholas Pert opts to retreat his queen back to safety, but this is the incorrect decision and after the game he was critical of this move. The point is that the queen on a4 does a good job on that square. In many lines it restricts Black's counterplay. For example, the queen attacks the bishop on a6, thus restricting the black queen. It also attacks the d7-square, so that after the inevitable ...♘bd7 the knight on f6 cannot move without leaving the other knight en prise. Thirdly, after ...♘bd7 White might have the option of playing ♕c6 in certain situations.

13 ♖b1! looks stronger, for example 13...♘bd7 14 e4 ♗xf1 15 ♔xf1 ♘h5 16 ♗d2 ♘e5 17 ♘xe5 ♗xe5 (Zarubin-Panchenko, Severodonetsk 1982). Black obviously has some compensation but it's unclear whether this is sufficient for the pawn deficit.

13...♘bd7 14 e3 ♘h5 15 ♗xa6?

This only helps Black's initiative. 15

g5 h6 16 ♗h4 is more resilient, although Black is still very active after 16...♖ab8.

15...♕xa6 16 ♗g5 h6 17 ♗h4 ♖ab8 18 ♕e2

Giving back the pawn in the hope of seeking salvation in the endgame. After the game Pert demonstrated the fantastic variation 18 g4 ♘f4!! 19 exf4

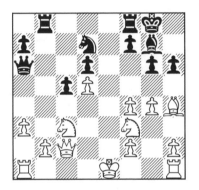

19...♖xb2!! 20 ♕xb2 ♕d3! and Black is clearly better after 21 ♕e2 (21 ♖c1 ♖e8+ 22 ♘e5 ♘xe5 23 ♕e2 ♘f3+ wins) 21...♕xc3+ 22 ♔f1 ♕xa1+ 23 ♔g2 ♕xa3.

18...♕xe2+ 19 ♘xe2 ♖xb2 20 ♖c1 ♖fb8

Black has regained his pawn and his initiative is no weaker despite the trade of queens. Probably White is already lost.

21 ♘g3 ♘hf6 22 ♗xf6 ♘xf6 23 0-0 ♖a2 24 e4 ♘d7 25 ♖b1 ♖b6 26 h3 ♖xa3 27 ♘d2 ♖a4 28 ♖bc1 ♖bb4 29 f4 ♗d4+ 30 ♔h1 ♖a3 31 ♔h2 ♖a2 32 ♘c4 ♘b6 33 ♘xd6 ♖bb2 34 ♖g1

Or 34 h4 ♖xg2+ 35 ♔h3 ♖h2+ 36 ♔g4 ♘d7! 37 e5 ♘b6 followed by ...♘xd5.

34...♗xg1+ 35 ♖xg1 c4 36 ♘f1 ♖a1 0-1

Black's c-pawn is a runner.

Exercise 4.2
A.Sokolov-Yusupov
Riga (1st match game) 1986
French Defence

(1 e4 e6 2 d4 d5 3 ♘c3 ♗b4 4 e5 c5 5 a3 ♗xc3+ 6 bxc3 ♘e7 7 ♘f3 b6 8 ♗b5+ ♗d7 9 ♗d3 ♗a4 10 h4 h6 11 h5 ♘bc6 12 ♖h4 c4 13 ♗e2) 13...♔d7!

A remarkable idea. The king plans to reach the relative safety of the queenside, but the real point is that Black intends ...♕g8-h7, when the queen finds a wonderful diagonal. I'm not sure, but I believe this was the first high-profile game where this concept was tried.

14 ♗e3 ♕g8 15 ♕d2 ♕h7 16 ♖c1 ♔c7

The queen is very well placed on h7, where it bears down on White's weak c2-pawn. Overall Black has good counter-chances here.

Exercise 5.1
Ljubojevic-Korchnoi
Brussels 1987

Yes, he can. The white king simply marches to the f7-square, after which White breaks through with g4-g5.

43 ♔g4 ♘f8 44 ♕d5!

A crucial move, preventing Black's defensive idea ...♘d7-e5.

44...♔h7 45 ♔f3 ♔h8 46 ♔e4 ♔h7 47 ♔d3 ♔h8 48 ♔c4 ♔h7 49 ♔b5 ♔h8 50 ♔c6 ♔h7 51 ♔c7 h5

Waiting doesn't help: 51...♔h8 52 ♔d8 ♔h7 53 ♔e8 ♔h8 54 ♔f7 ♔h7 55 g4 ♔h8 56 g5 hxg5 57 hxg5 fxg5 58 ♕h1+ ♘h7 59 ♔g6 and White wins.

52 ♔d8 ♔h6 53 ♔e8 1-0

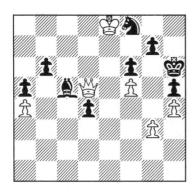

Black resigned on account of 53...♔h7 54 ♔f7 ♔h6 (54...♔h8 55 ♕f3; 54...d3 55 ♕f3 ♔h6 56 ♔g8! and ♕b7) 55 ♔g8! ♘h7 56 ♕f7 and White mates.

Exercise 5.2
Karpov-M.Gurevich
Reggio Emilia 1991

No is the answer. After 73...♕d7+ 74 ♔g2 White is only slightly better.
73...♕xe4?
Now White has a forced win:
74 ♗xd4! exd4 75 ♕f7+ ♔h6 76 ♕f8+ ♔h5 77 ♕h8+ ♗h6

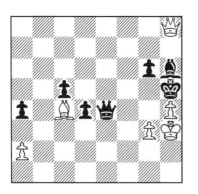

All forced, but what now?
78 ♕e5+!! 1-0
It's mate after 78...♕xe5 79 g4 or 78...g5 79 ♗f7+ ♕g6 80 g4.

Exercise 6.1
Sakaev-S.Ivanov
Moscow 2003

28 ♖d6!
Occupying the outpost immediately gives White a winning position. Now if Black does nothing White's winning plan is ♖fd1, ♕g8 and then ♘h7-f6+, so Black is forced to capture on d6.
28...♖xd6 29 exd6 ♕xd6
Or 29...♕d7 30 ♖d1!, intending ♕g8 followed by ♘h7.
30 ♕xf7+ ♔d8 31 ♕b7! ♕d5 32 ♘xe6+! ♕xe6 33 ♕xa8+ ♔e7 34 ♕a7+ ♘d7 35 ♖d1 1-0

Exercise 6.2
Ionescu-Kengis
Timisoara 1987

(1 d4 ♘f6 2 c4 e6 3 ♘f3 b6 4 ♘c3 ♗b7 5 ♗g5 h6 6 ♗h4 ♗b4 7 ♕c2 g5 8 ♗g3 ♘e4 9 e3 ♗xc3+ 10 bxc3 ♘xg3 11 hxg3 ♘c6)
12 ♖h5!
A good use of rook power, preventing ...h6-h5, threatening the immediate ♘xg5 and nailing down the h6-pawn as a weakness.
12...♕f6 13 g4!
Cementing the bind on the kingside. Now White will follow up with ♘d2 and ♗e2-f3 with a pleasant edge.